ZONE MIND,
ZONE BODY

How to break through to new levels of
fitness and performance – by doing less!

Roy Palmer

ecademy-press.com

Zone Mind, Zone Body

ISBN 1-905823-06-1
978-1-905823-06-2

Cover Design: JuiceCreative
Layout design and setting: Jaquetta Trueman
Book text set in 11pt Abadi Regular

First published in 2006 by Ecademy Press

Contact:
Ecademy Press
6, Woodland Rise
Penryn, Cornwall, UK
TR10 8QD

info@ecademy-press.com

Printed and Bound by Lightning Source UK and USA

Acknowledgements

This book would not have been written without the help from Mindy Gibbins-Klein. From its inception through to the result you see here, she has helped me every step along the way. I doubt I would have finished this project without her. Huge thanks to Angela Sherman for reading the drafts, painstakingly pointing out all the missing commas and writing the promotional copy. Her feedback and support was most encouraging and much appreciated.

Thanks also to my 'models' Scott Brown and especially Sophie Webber for their amazing patience whilst I fiddled with my camera for the twentieth retake – they were great.

I would also like to express gratitude to my regular pupils Alyson Greenstone, Di Whelan, Joyce Makepeace and Scott Brown who have had to endure listening to my endless theories over the months. Their feedback and continued support are most appreciated.

As they say, I wouldn't be here today without... the guidance and training from all the Alexander teachers at The Alexander Re-education Centre. A special thanks for the work of Ron Colyer and Ray Evans, who sadly passed away recently. I know I would not be running if it wasn't for the instruction from Malcolm Balk who applies this remarkable technique with such enthusiasm.

Thanks to Kris Akabusi, Greg Chappell, Annabel Meade, Joel Grant-Jones and Phil Pask for their time, input, feedback and encouragement.

And finally, to my wife, Bernadette, and my children, Timothy and Neve, who provided me with the motivation and inspiration to see this project to the end.

Contents

Foreword

Frederick Matthias Alexander discovered the link between thought and tension in the body. By changing the way he thought while carrying out certain actions he was able to improve his performance and, subsequently, the performance of those whom he taught.

Roy Palmer in his book Zone Mind, Zone Body explains in a straightforward and entertaining manner how anyone can improve their performance by understanding that their intention and their thought processes can either hinder or help their performance.

Zone Mind, Zone Body will show the professional athlete, or the weekend warrior, that working harder is not necessarily the best solution to any problem. By changing the thought process and the understanding of what constitutes efficient movement, performance can be improved almost instantaneously.

This book will be a very useful addition to the tool kit of any coach or performer.

Gregory Stephen Chappell MBE
Former Australian Cricket Captain and
current Indian National Cricket Coach

Introduction

Have you ever achieved the performance of your life while experiencing the feeling that it was effortless? That everything you tried worked to perfection? If you have experienced this, you were in The Zone.

The Zone has achieved mystical status in the world of sport and it is not surprising to see why. It's a paradox. How can a peak performance be achieved with such little perceived effort? Surely if we are working at the very limits of our ability it should be hard work and not feel like a stroll in the park?

This book looks at what may be happening when we are in The Zone, and why experiencing it remains both a rare and unpredictable occurrence – and for many, completely unobtainable. Accounts from athletes, combined with studies conducted on the subject, not only give us vital clues to what this mysterious state is; but more importantly, they may show us how to get there more often.

The procedures in this book will give you a totally different sensation of movement and show you how to take control of previously hidden factors influencing your performance. The methods I use are based on The Alexander Technique, the world-renowned system for developing what I call intelligence in action. My hope is that by creating a subtle shift in your thinking, you will be able to recognise aspects of your training that may be keeping you out of The Zone.

This book is the result of ten years of experimenting, observing and applying the Alexander principles to my own sports of martial arts and running and also working with sports people in other fields. One surprising fact I have observed during this time is that, regardless of ability or experience, many people use their bodies in a way that interferes with their natural coordination. The procedures here will help you identify whether or not this is true for you. I am not going to use exercises in the usual accepted sense, because I believe they serve only to encourage the sort of habits that cause this and ulti-mately keep you out of The Zone. Besides, how many more types of exercise do we need to learn? Do we really benefit from doing all these actions that have little in common with those of our sport, or, for that matter everyday natural movements?

In addition to identifying habits that may be holding you back, my procedures can also help you to understand what it is that makes you good at what you do. You may have a 'natural talent' for your sport but if you are not consciously aware of which attributes give you this ability, what happens if injury intervenes? It is common for athletes to struggle to recover form after injury because if they don't know what enabled them to achieve that form in the first place. How do they get it back?

I believe conventional methods of sports training and exercise, in which we have placed our trust entirely, could be preventing the essential balanced state necessary for entering The Zone. I propose it is time to move on from the view that performance can be improved by simply trying harder or spending a high proportion of valuable training time on exercise drills. Instead, we need to develop a more creative, mindful approach to our training. Ask most athletes how they entered The Zone and you will get a shrug of the shoulders. Is this not evidence that, even at the top level, there is still an element of the unknown in relation to human activity?

Perhaps the way to The Zone lies in developing our skills of self-awareness above and beyond our current ability. A departure from current ideas may allow us to discover new areas of previously untapped resources that would give us more control over our performance, leaving less to chance or circumstances beyond our current understanding. The skills you can learn from this book can be applied to any activity – adding a vital new resource to your existing abilities.

If you are used to vigorous forms of training then at first this way may seem a little pedestrian. However, if you can suspend judgment for the duration of this book you may find that this subtle, yet powerful approach is one of the best ways to focus and enhance your performance.

Marc Salem, Professor of Psychology, offers some very useful advice to all of us: *"Minds are like parachutes; they only work when they are open"*.

1 | Into the Unknown

Success at sport can be unpredictable. On some days you may feel completely in control and sink that difficult putt or run the perfect race with total confidence in your ability and judgement. On other days, nothing goes right. The simple becomes impossible; you feel clumsy and incapable of carrying out your usual activities. It's as if your talent has deserted you. This has always puzzled me. How could I apply my skills so effectively one moment, only to become totally incompetent the next? When my poor performances became more frequent and began to outnumber the good days, I decided to take action.

In common with most athletes, I suffered from injuries. But even when I was fully fit, my form remained erratic. Examining my experiences at both ends of the performance spectrum highlighted one main difference: it was how I moved, or more accurately, how the movement felt. On a good day, I felt light. My body was so quick to react to my wishes, I felt I was ahead of the game. In contrast, when my form dipped, I experienced a heaviness and apparent reluctance for spontaneous action. An average performance would be somewhere in between. Perhaps it should have been obvious to me; but because I was totally preoccupied with the what, getting the right result, I was unaware of the how.

Sounds ridiculous, doesn't it? However working with other athletes over the last ten years has shown that I was by no means unique.

So what determined the standard of my performance, and what

could account for the gradual deterioration? At this point I was in my mid-twenties and had just been awarded a karate black belt, so I reasoned it could not be my age. Surely with experience and regular practice I should be getting better and was still a long way from my peak. Months of experimenting with diet and training drills had very little impact. This is not to say nutrition and training are not important, but in my case I was convinced they were not the cause.

There was another as yet unknown factor influencing the quality of my performance.

Eventually, I found an answer to my dilemma that would radically change my attitude to sport and physical activity. It came from an unexpected source. Whilst trying to resolve a long-standing back problem, I came upon the Alexander Technique. At my first lesson, the teacher pointed out something I was doing that made movement much harder than it should be. This 'something' resulted in using far too much effort to carry out even simple activities – and yet I wasn't even aware I was doing it! This came as quite a shock.

I had mistakenly thought that my years of running, swimming and karate training, whilst achieving respectable results, should have taught me at least how to move efficiently. Apparently not. In my case I had spent that time learning to do things badly and the longer I trained, the better I got at doing things badly. My situation had deteriorated because the poor habits I had unknowingly developed resulted in poor movement, which in turn conditioned my muscles in a way that led to yet more inefficient movement. It was a vicious circle and as my standard of movement declined, so did my appreciation and memory of what good movement actually felt like. Whoever said 'practice makes permanent, not necessarily perfect' must have had me in mind.

So now I had an answer. In an instant my teacher could show me what I needed to stop doing in order to allow my body to move more easily. By using her hands she could get me to move with the lightness I associated with a peak performance. Problem solved, I thought.

Well, actually it was the just beginning – because there is this considerable barrier called habit. Habit determines how we do just about everything, yet we are practically oblivious of its presence and hence its influence. When asked to stop tightening my neck, shoulders and back just to get out of a chair, without my Alexander teacher's hands to guide me, I found I could not. When asked to take a step forward without collapsing into the supporting leg, I found I could not. If I could not carry out these basic activities that make up the building blocks of all human movement, how could I trust in my ability to perform the complex techniques of my sport? Not a chance.

Try the following experiment and you will see why changing a habit can be difficult.

1   Fold your arms, note the position of your hands and which arm is on the outside.

2   Now unfold them and fold them again, but this time the opposite way. Note your reaction to how this feels.

Does it feel odd, or even wrong? In the first step you used your habitual 'folding the arms' pattern. You did not have to think about how you did it because you have an existing pattern; it's automatic and feels right. Did you have to think for a moment before carrying out the second instruction? It may even have taken several attempts to achieve. This is because you do not have an existing pattern for this movement and it has to be consciously worked out. It will probably feel wrong because you will not have done it like this before so the sensations from the muscles and joints will be new to you. The important lesson from this experiment is how the two positions feel. Your habitual pattern feels right and is easy to do, your non-habitual opposite way feels wrong and is not quite so easy to do. There is obviously nothing wrong with the opposite arm-fold, but it will feel wrong. What feels right and wrong is therefore determined by habits that may be working for you – but also against you.

REALITY CHECK

How you think, move and the actions you take are ruled by your habits that feel right. You would not usually perform a move that feels wrong – certainly not in the heat of competition. So if all your training and practice is done because of the way it feels, your progress will be limited by the boundaries dictated by your existing habitual patterns. The next time you want to fold your arms, see if you can change the pattern, go into the unknown, and fold them the opposite way. You will invariably find your arms are already folded before you have had chance to try the opposite, non-habitual way. This represents the challenge you are up against when you want to raise your performance, because obviously you will try to do it right. This means you are really doing it in a way that feels familiar because you have done it like this thousands of times before. You may have an excellent and reliable technique but the fact remains you are led by your habits.

The Enemy Within

Scientific research shows that our brains virtually ignore sensations that are familiar or expected – this explains why we cannot tickle ourselves. Modern training techniques emphasize the importance of feedback for performance enhancement; yet if your habitual patterns dominate, this process is drastically undermined. Your brain will ignore the familiar signals coming back from your body and make it difficult to monitor what is happening. Some experiments later in this book will help to demonstrate this fact and how it can restrict progress.

Habits act as boundaries that limit not only how you move but also your concept of movement. You will need to learn how to move outside these boundaries, or to be dramatic, go into the unknown, in order to take your performance to a higher level. I am not aware of any training method in sport, whether classed 'mental' or 'physical,' that encompasses this fundamental aspect of human behaviour. Consequently such methods can only achieve results within your existing habitual patterns.

Are your habits having a detrimental affect on your movement? How would you know? Nature has not given you the necessary equipment to ring a bell when you are performing below your optimum level – although you may become aware of the consequences, such as injury.

When I tried to get out of a chair without getting set by stiffening my neck, shoulders and back, I could not do it because it did not feel right to do it any other way. I would not attempt to even start the movement before I had set up the tension I felt necessary to prepare. So even though these actions made the movement less efficient, my habitual 'getting out of the chair' pattern dictated otherwise.

I quickly appreciated that my whole concept of movement and effort was wrong, and that all my activities were carried out with the same poor habitual patterns. In short, I had lost the art of natural movement and with it, all hope of retaining the sort of performance of which I had once been capable. Perhaps I even had deteriorated to the point where I would have to give up my sport.

The Smart Zone

However, here is the good news – it is possible to learn how to step beyond these performance-limiting habits and exceed your expectations. This is the purpose of the procedures in this book, and we shall approach it by looking at the ultimate experience for any athlete known as The Zone.

Perhaps you have had the occasional awe-inspiring moments of being in The Zone? These surpass everything else by some distance and every detail can be recalled with ease long after the event. I believe this state is an inborn function, a sort of higher state we can enter when necessary. But if this is true, why are our moments in The Zone rare, brief, and as often reported, achieved by accident?

I think the clue lies in the unlooked for and accidental way in which many find themselves entering The Zone. Rather than doing something consciously to reach it, perhaps for a moment we unconsciously let go of those habitual patterns that keep us out of it. My journey involved recognising these actions that took me further away from my optimum natural state (that paradoxically were induced by an exercise culture meant to improve fitness and function.) I began to question why I spent more time doing 'exercise' than I did participating in my sporting activities. Would my karate and running be enhanced doing sit-ups, leg raises and workouts at the gym? They had nothing in common with the movements of my sport. Do you spend the majority of your training away from your sport? Have you ever questioned whether you get any real benefit from these exercises that are supposed to help your sports performance?

I propose that instead of training harder to improve performance, you can learn to train smarter and consciously create the conditions that will allow you to reach The Zone. Your performance will then take care of itself, risk of injury is considerably reduced and you will learn more about yourself and your sport in the process.

Conclusion

Underpinning all your actions are habits. Due to their nature they remain concealed; slowly they can corrupt your performance and, worse still, your sense of movement, not unlike an undetected virus lurking in the depths of your computer. Remarkably, we trust these habits entirely and resist any attempt to change them. And you will; just wait until you try some of the experiments in this book! Yet if we can discard these habits and the ideas that go with them, the results can be remarkable.

If you want to take your sport to a higher level you will by definition have to venture into the unknown. This means going to new places you don't yet know. Keep in mind that you cannot achieve what you don't yet know purely by doing what you do know.

2 Defining The Elusive Zone

To witness an athlete performing in The Zone is a joy. It may be Michael Johnson coming out of the last bend leaving the rest standing, or Muhammad Ali, who really could float like a butterfly, dancing around the ring. Such performances transcend spectator loyalties to be appreciated by all. Athletes performing at their peak can be inspirational, as they demonstrate the potential we all have in us. Whilst watching an athlete in The Zone is a pleasure, to actually perform in it is sublime. Few lifetime experiences can surpass the moment when years of practice come to a peak and everything seems to flow. But what exactly is The Zone? Why do we derive such pleasure from it, both as a spectator and participant?

How often have you been in The Zone? Can you remember what you did to get there? The purpose of this chapter is to build a picture of The Zone based on the experience of athletes, plus neuroscience, and research by sports scientists. If we can understand the processes involved and why we have developed this capacity, we could increase our chances of getting there.

The Zone is the holy grail of sport. Athletes who experience it describe it as the ultimate state, a sort of nirvana, a pinnacle of achievement to reach and enjoy. It is often portrayed as a mysterious, altered state where performance is effortless, trouble-free and near to perfection. Many feel they can anticipate events, permitting them to take action before their opponent. The stress and anxiety of performing vanishes leaving them free to function without fear of consequences.

Another commonly reported phenomenon is the nature in which The Zone is experienced: usually, it occurs unexpectedly. Athletes will suddenly find themselves in it. Then as soon as they acknowledge it, they lose it. Those who do feel able to enter it at will are generally elite athletes and even in these cases it occurs more often during training than in competition.

Since the late 1970s there has been a number of studies into The Zone. However researchers have found it difficult to measure and classify something as subjective as a feeling. Often their subjects would struggle to put into words what they actually felt while in The Zone. Can we express ourselves thoroughly enough to give an accurate picture of what may be happening in these circumstances? To appreciate the difficulty of investigating such phenomena, try to describe what happiness feels like. Not what makes you happy, but what do you actually experience in yourself when you're happy? Or how do you know when you are happy?

Dr Kenneth Ravizza, a sports psychologist, conducted one of the earliest studies into The Zone in 1979. In his paper titled, *A subjective study of the athlete's greatest moment in sport* he surmised their experience was,

> " ... *temporary and of relatively short duration; non-voluntary and not induced at will; and unique."*

He found that it required many years of practice and experience before they were capable of entering it. In subsequent studies Ravizza described being in The Zone as,

> "... *a merging of the player's actions and awareness, centering of higher attention, loss of personal ego, control of personal action and the external environment, demands for action and clear feedback, and an intrinsic reward system."*

He went on to define three categories of peak experiences as (1) focused awareness, (2) having complete control of self and the environment and (3) transcendence of the self.

In 1999 Young and Pain from Monash University, Melbourne, Australia published *The Zone: Evidence of a universal phenomenon for athletes across sport*. Their research revealed that regardless of the sport, athletes appeared to experience the same 'heightened state of consciousness'. Taking into account the limitations of language when describing such experiences, participants repeatedly used words such as peak, perfect moments, mindfulness and flow.

Perhaps the most well known writer on the subject of The Zone is Mihaly Csikszentmihalyi, a professor of psychology. He describes it as,

> *"being completely involved in an activity for its own sake. The ego falls away. Time flies. Every action, movement, and thought follows inevitably from the previous one, like playing jazz. Your whole being is involved, and you're using your skills to the utmost."*

Michael Jordan, one of basketball's greatest talents, described one particular game where everything he attempted worked; it was too easy and felt he could do no wrong. But as soon as he thought to himself, 'I must be in The Zone,' it was gone.

When Sebastian Coe broke the 800-metre world record in Oslo 1979 he said afterwards,

> *"I thought I might get somewhere near the European record of 1:43.70. I had no particular sensation of speed, and I think I could have run even faster. I wasn't exhausted at all in the end."*

He actually recorded of time of 1:42.33, beating the previous record by a huge margin of 1.1 seconds; a record that stood for 16 years. Coe had run the race of his life as if it was a jog in the park. If you watch a recording of the race you can see the disbelief on his face as he sees the clock at the finish line. Coe was in complete command from start to finish; he felt relaxed, and despite the world record-breaking performance had 'no particular sensation of speed'. He has since said that if he had been aware of the time at the end of the first lap it probably would have changed his tactics – and the course of the race – for the worse.

A review of the studies completed to date identifies seven common characteristics described by athletes in The Zone:

1 They are totally absorbed and focused on the activity.

2 They experience an inner clarity and understand exactly what is required of them, knowing their skills are perfectly matched to the task.

3 They have a sense of ecstasy, being outside everyday reality.

4 They describe 'being in the moment' focusing completely on the present; unaware of time passing but conversely, they have a sense of time slowing down.

5 They feel a deep passion for the activity, driving them on to higher levels of performance. This experience provides further inspiration; it becomes self-perpetuating.

6 They have a sense of serenity, no anxiety, no ego – consequently no fear about performance.

7 They experience no sense of effort. The activity becomes almost easy and feels like they are 'getting out of the way' of their performance.

The Flintstone Connection

Before studying these in more depth let's look at The Zone in a wider sense. What is this ability that allows us to function beyond our normal everyday capacity? What evolutionary purpose does it serve? Is it a primitive ability? Have the comforts of modern civilisation rendered it obsolete, or does The Zone represent the next stage in our evolution – a sort of higher state of consciousness?

The Zone is not restricted to the world of sport. It's a reported phenomenon in the creative and performing arts, more commonly referred to as 'The Flow'. You may also enter this altered state whilst cutting the grass, playing with your children, listening to music or even whilst doing nothing. Practitioners of Zen can alter their state of mind just by sitting in zazen, a form of meditation.

I believe our capacity to enter The Zone state is an ability we share with animals, originating from a primitive survival skill that heightens our state of alertness in hazardous situations. Whether you're the hunter or the hunted, an awareness of your surroundings is crucial to carrying out your survival directive. A hunter poised with his spear waiting for the right moment to strike needs to be mindful of his prey's intentions, yet he cannot afford to concentrate solely on the animal. He will need to remain aware of other sounds and movements around him. These could include the actions of a bigger, hungrier animal; the position of his fellow hunters; and the conditions of the immediate terrain. In addition to the external events, he has to keep breathing and avoid unnecessary tension, so he's ready when the time comes to attack. Our hunter cannot afford to focus purely on the target at the expense of shutting out valuable input from other senses that might yet prove crucial.

Perhaps being in The Zone was a common experience for our ancestors in the course of their daily survival activities. If we look at the seven Zone characteristics listed earlier I would say that all could apply to our hunter. Although if they hadn't eaten for several days, then conceivably they would experience some interest in the outcome – possibly to the extent of becoming anxious if their hunt was not going to plan.

Survivors of near-death experiences often report changes in their perceptual abilities judged to be critical to their escape. For example, their sense of touch and special awareness become more acute when they're attempting to find their way out of smoke-filled rooms.

Another common phenomenon in such circumstances is seeing their 'life flashing before their eyes' in the moments anticipating death. In his book 'Neural Networks and Fuzzy Logic', Bart Kosko proposes this could be the mind frantically searching its memory in an attempt to find a solution to the present predicament. Feats of amazing endurance or trials of strength when desperate measures are called for, suggest a human capacity for going beyond 'normal' limitations. In a number of near-death situations some report that acceptance of their perceived fate brings relief and a strange unexplained calmness, even joy. Again if we look at The Zone characteristics, a number could be applicable here, although it's probably not advisable to use this route to achieve it!

Modern sport could be seen as an evolvement of our ancient survival and hunting skills. Aside from the obvious archery and shooting and their connection to hunting, all sports require speed, skill and intelligence greater than your opponent if you are to win or 'survive'. Some see sport as the next step up from warfare, where the pride of a nation's youth can compete against each other for honour without the need for fatalities. Could engaging ourselves in the old skills take us back to The Zone? But how can less competitive activities such as art, sitting in silence or playing with the children get us into the flow? With the exception of the latter, they could not be viewed as situations requiring our utmost survival skills.

Perhaps creativity is an essential element of our instincts that helps us to seek out solutions to complex survival issues? Creativity also plays a part in sport. Being able to out-think your opponent requires creative and original thought. Could The Zone state be a merging of an instinctive skill with the more recently evolved functions of our analytical conscious mind?

The Zone Experience

Although studies find similarities in athletes' descriptions of The Zone, there are notable differences. For instance, in my interviews with athletes some reported being fully aware of the sound coming from spectators and even their appearance – whilst others seemed to register nothing beyond the immediate field of competition. Perhaps some individuals need to feel the encouragement of the supporters to raise their performance whereas others would see this as a distraction.

New Zealand rugby phenomenon Jona Lomu was asked what he thought about once he had got the ball and was heading for the line. Did he focus on the line as if nothing could stop him? Lomu replied that for him it was the exact opposite; he had to be aware of every player on the pitch, where they were and which direction they were heading. He described it as being 'hyper alert' to his surroundings.

If we look at the seven zone characteristics in more detail we can discover what may be happening on both physiological and psychological levels. Although we can explore these individually I believe they are all interconnected and, if you experience one, invariably the others will be present.

Zone Characteristic 1:
Being totally absorbed and focused on the activity.

From my own experience, being 'focused on the activity' does not mean that to the detriment of everything else. Being in The Zone is not being so absorbed in your activity to the point you get run over by an unseen truck! This would be prolonged concentration, which in my mind, is a narrowing of awareness and the opposite to the desired alert state of The Zone. Whilst periods of concentration are necessary for peak performance, they should only be for the duration for each immediate task so we can return to a state of general awareness, alert to everything happening around us. We will look at this on more detail shortly.

Do we have to be interested to become absorbed? Earlier I mentioned it was possible to enter The Zone whilst performing seemingly mundane tasks such as mowing the lawn. One of my responsibilities whilst living at home with my parents was to cut the grass. As an activity it could not be described as being up there with football or cricket; in fact it was a huge inconvenience to a sports-mad teenager. Yet I have vivid memories of one hot August afternoon, being totally absorbed in the simple act of pushing the mower up and down the lawn. I even finished off the edges with the shears and took great pride in the straightness of the lines and neatness around the borders. So what was happening here? Csikszentmihalyi's studies of athletes, performing artists, chess players and factory workers found that we can derive great pleasure when totally focused on a task, even if it is quite mundane. He concluded that if four specific criteria are met it is possible for us to enter what he refers to as The

Flow. They are:

i. The presence of a challenging activity

ii. The perception that your skills match the challenge

iii. Clear goals

iv. The availability of instant feedback concerning your performance

In most sporting activities these elements are present, allowing you to become totally immersed in the activity for its own sake. It is also clear that other pursuits, such as the performing arts and also manual tasks, can provide the same conditions for involving the individual. In my early Zone experience, cutting the grass was a challenging activity as the mower was ancient and not easy to push, but I knew from experience that I was capable of completing it. The goals were clear and at every turn I could see instantly the results of my work as another perfectly straight-mown stripe of lawn appeared. This changed the activity from a repetitive task into a pleasurable one as I face the challenge of reproducing the desired result. When I reluctantly started the task I hadn't viewed it as challenge or even tried to make it interesting; it just turned out that way as I become captivated in the act of doing it.

It is easy to see how we can become absorbed in our sport; but also, perhaps we begin to appreciate how we can make it difficult. Any thoughts likely to distract us from the task in hand will prevent the focus necessary for a Zone experience. As we shall discuss later these include obvious thoughts, such as anxiety about performance; also, less apparent, are thoughts of trying too hard and applying the wrong kind of effort. I believe the harder we try to focus the more likely we are to interfere with the process. But perhaps the most important aspect is what activity do we focus on? It may sound obvious to focus on your running for example, but as we shall see later this is not as clear as it initially appears.

Zone Characteristic 2:
Experience of an inner clarity and understanding exactly what is required, knowing their skills are matched to the task.

From my own experience of The Zone this can also be thought of as economy of effort. Absolutely nothing is irrelevant to the task, both mentally and physically. Every thought is pertinent to the situation resulting in a purposeful, minimal and appropriate act. A glance at a thesaurus for entries on clarity finds clearness, lucidity, simplicity and precision. If we are to understand exactly what is required and how to do it, we need to be totally alert to what is happening; translate this raw data into usable information; evaluate it based on previous experience and then act in a way we decide is the most appropriate.

This cycle is a continuous process, of which we are generally unaware; but during Zone moments something appears to change. I believe the change is that we become conscious of the process but we are not directly doing or controlling it – it's a sort of detached state. The closest comparison I can think of is that of the role of a ship's captain. The captain receives information from the crew and gives the command for something to happen. All the work relating to the command is delegated and carried out elsewhere. The captain doesn't have to get his hands dirty shovelling coal in the engine room. Indeed, it would reduce the effectiveness of his command if he did.

The sense of clarity and simplicity athletes experience comes when they become totally focused on the present and do not need to worry about how they perform. It's as if the whole self quietens down; the usual nervous system traffic between the brain and body is reduced because you're no longer distracted by irrelevant thoughts.

Turn on, tune in, Zone out

How do our senses determine relevance? If we consciously decide what to focus our attention on, could we miss something small that turns out to be significant? Or could we focus wrongly on inconsequential factors? Although our senses are constantly active, we are conscious of only a small percentage of what they detect. There are billions of signals travelling between the body and brain at any one moment. It would not be possible to function if we were distracted by the workings of every bodily function. Priority is given to signals reporting an exception to the 'business as usual' circumstances.

For instance, when running we do not need to know what the left hamstring muscles are doing so long as they contract and release at the right time. The signals travelling to and from this area are dealt with at a level in our brain below consciousness. However, if one of these muscles develops a problem, we become conscious of it immediately because we will need to take action. The exceptional signals coming from this damaged muscle pass through a filtering system to reach higher up into our brain – to a point where we become aware of a problem. The captain needs to make a decision! The system that filters and directs signals is called the Reticular Activating System (RAS), a collection of structures in the lower part of the brain linked up into the higher levels associated with consciousness.

It is known that memory plays a role in what we selectively pay attention to, because certain things will have become more important through past experience. Scientists refer to a process called the 'cocktail party phenomenon' that not only describes how this system functions, but also gives us an interesting insight into a scientist's social life! Even if you have never been to a cocktail party you will probably have experienced the phenomenon. In a crowded, noisy room you can focus on what a particular individual is saying. It is even possible to filter out surrounding sounds to pick up on a conversation on the other side of the room. During your conversation you may suddenly hear a specific word over the general background noise, triggering you attention. This trigger may be your name or another word that holds a personal interest such as your sport or team. The most common trigger is the word 'sex.' Try saying this in a crowded room; you won't have to shout it. Even if it's said in a normal voice you will see many heads turn. Although you have been engaged in another activity, your senses are still monitoring everything in that room in case something important happens. When something does happens that exceeds the 'relevance threshold' the information is passed higher up to your conscious level.

The significance of this phenomenon is that if you tried to monitor every conversation in that room, you could only focus on one at a time and would be incapable of holding a proper conversation. If you have tried to listen to the game on the radio whilst pretending you are listening to your partner, you will appreciate the difficulty. The next time you are playing in a team sport, try consciously to note where every player in the game is located and see how difficult it is to 'do' it. Yet if you allow yourself to become absorbed and enjoy the game, you will be in a better state to register players and their position and their relevance to the run of play. Experience of your sport will allow you to monitor unconsciously what is and what isn't relevant for a particular situation.

I believe the greater inner clarity associated with The Zone is a result of 'getting out of the way' to allow natural abilities, evolved over millions of years, to function properly. Again, this could explain how we can suddenly find ourselves in this state without feeling we have done anything to get there. So possibly we don't have to do anything specific; we just need to stop doing whatever we are doing that is preventing us attaining it. This shall be discussed in the next chapter.

The Zone is also known as The Flow due to the sensation that thoughts flow freely into actions. A number of studies have found that athletes performing at their peak are able to shift attention rapidly across many external events.

The neurotransmitter dopamine, produced when we need to 'switch on' for a task, is known to create this effect. The increased speed of brain processing allows large volumes of incoming data to be analysed. Data is compared against memories of similar situations to determine what is and what isn't appropriate to the task. Incoming sensations that are new and have yet to be proved useful would find no 'match' in our memory, and therefore would not be acted upon. What we actually experience may only be a fraction of all this activity because only the pertinent, processed results are passed up to a conscious level after we have already reacted. In situations like these we often use the term 'reflex' to describe the experience that it all happened without the need for us to intervene.

An athlete on the last lap looking at the back of the leader will know she can only win by increasing her pace. She knows this because in the past when she has done it she has won. A more experienced athlete will probably know the strengths and weakness of the runner in front and be better placed to select the right moment to make her move. Of course there will be many runners on the track all of which need to be included in the equation of when to go for it. Each runner's movements are noted and their actions and impact on the race as a whole are considered. Our runner has to be careful not to concentrate entirely on one aspect of the race, as other vital information may be missed. A sudden movement of a runner at her shoulder needs to be registered, its relevance assessed, and appropriate action taken. As soon as this is done she needs to determine the impact of her action, and return to general awareness mode in order to receive more data.

When a runner loses a race and reports that the winner 'came from nowhere', they were obviously not in The Zone. An alert athlete would have heard the approaching competitor or have been aware of events beyond the immediate track such as the response from the spectators anticipating a close finish.

Once you have an accurate understanding of what is happening, you still have to decide the best, most appropriate action. Ravizza's research found that Zone experiences tend to follow on from years of practice. Chances of an appropriate response increase as the memory store (your repertoire) of a particular sport becomes larger, containing many variations. In a heightened state triggered by dopamine release, your memories can be scanned rapidly for a match. The learned pattern selected for the moment can be executed close to perfection if there is no anxiety about the outcome. Negative responses to stress will impede the free-flowing feel of action associated with The Zone. The higher rate of processing may also account for the sense of time slowing down – that is, more happening in a shorter time – and the impression of having longer to make decisions while in The Zone.

Zone Characteristic 3:
A sense of ecstasy – being outside everyday reality.

As discussed earlier I believe being in The Zone is an inborn ability. So, the sensation of 'being outside everyday reality' is in my view an experience of the real thing – what life should be like. Everyday reality may be our normal state of living but this can be well below our natural optimum degree of functioning. This invariably means switching between the extremes of concentration (a narrowing of awareness) and a dream-like state (turning off awareness to retreat internally), neither of which are conducive to a Zone experience. (Note the use of *natural* and *normal* and that normal does not necessarily mean natural.)

Where does the sense of ecstasy come from? We take it for granted that to perform well is satisfying or to do something that surpasses all else is sublime, but why should this lead to feelings of elation? What structures in the brain produce this sensation and why do we have this function?

Neuroscientist and Nobel Prize winner, Gerald Edelman, proposes that the brain has a built-in system that allows us to learn from experience and to reinforce 'good' survival behaviour. He believes this skill is essential if we are to adapt to, and exist in, whichever of the world's contrasting environments into which we may be born.

Edelman argues that his theory '*allows the brain to optimally adapt to the local physical and cultural environment.*' It does this by evaluating outcomes. When an action produces a good result, for instance continued survival, the active connections in the brain at that moment are strengthened – whilst non-active connections are weakened for that situation. When you pull off that perfect shot, your brain has the ability to 'remember' what was happening at that moment. Edelman uses the phrase '*nerves that fire together wire together*'. This process enables us to learn appropriate behaviour for specific circumstances based on experience. If we find ourselves in a totally new situation, the process starts again until a good result is achieved. It is a trial and error system that develops strong connections which survive whilst the weakest are lost; hence the name Edelman applied to his theory – Neural Darwinism. However, this process can also work against us, as we shall see later in this book.

But how do we know what is good or bad behaviour? How does the brain of a newborn baby with no experience of the outside world determine the difference? Here Edelman suggests that a group of cells in the brainstem and hypothalamus (the centre controlling body temperature, thirst, hunger etc), provides a 'value system' to guide behaviour and consequently development. Millions of years of evolution's trial and error method has resulted in an organism that 'knows' which circumstances are better suited to its survival. Many scientists believe this process is the basis for emotion. Nature had to develop a mechanism that would produce an urge to act that's hard to ignore – a bit like an uncompromising sports coach. You may not feel like doing what they are asking, but deep down you know they are right and you have no choice!

Let's return to the question of newborn babies. Their brains are guided by primitive emotional functions; these know that to be warm is better than to be cold, to be dry is better than wet, that a full stomach is better than an empty one, and so on. These are matters of survival and an infant will cry when these needs are not being met. I also believe that the brain 'knows' it is better to be active than still in the first few years as movement allows the brain-body connections to be made. Ultimately, survival will depend on mobility and being capable of basic everyday functions. Yet at birth, the connections from the muscles do not yet reach the higher centres of the brain that would enable intentional movement. Paradoxically these connections cannot be made until the muscles become active, so enabling developing nerves from the brain and the muscle to link up. The primitive reflexes present in the lower centres of the newborn's brain contain patterns to kick start movement. These force the connections to a higher level, giving the conscious part of the brain access to the muscles. It's only when these connections are made that we can begin to learn what thoughts move which limb and in which direction.

This process takes many months and again is a trial and error method. Our chances of survival increase as we learn more about the outside world through action and observation. This could also explain why, as young children, we enjoy repetitive games and nursery rhymes that help us learn to predict outcome and give us sequences that help consolidate our understanding of the world.

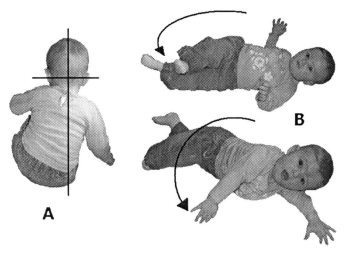

Fig 2.1 Early reflex activity initiates movements to develop balance and coordination skills for life. Repetition of stereotyped movements helps to build pathways between the brain and muscle. (A) The head-righting reflex coordinates muscle activity to maintain balance. (B) The segmental rolling reflexes coordinate cross-lateral activities such as walking, running and swimming.

So how does this relate to the sense of ecstasy an athlete experiences in The Zone? What basic requirements are met to produce this reward? If you have had the pleasure of seeing a young child walk for the first time, you can appreciate the reward movement can bring by watching his or her face. As we mature other skills associated with survival develop. Beyond the basic needs of being well fed and comfortable, more complex needs arise such as being valued, loved and respected. For instance, a successful athlete is held in high esteem by people who aspire to be like her. She is able to demonstrate the potential we have to use our skill to its utmost, achieving remarkable feats of balance, coordination, anticipation and judgement. The acclaim and acknowledgment from her peers confirms status whilst re-enforcing the value of her behaviour – that is, what she does that makes her a good athlete.

Perhaps, then, the sense of ecstasy we can experience in The Zone is the result of our primeval urge to survive through the acquisition of skills. Edelman's 'value system' is fired into action to consolidate this desirable behaviour, and temporarily we live life at a higher level fulfilling our main purpose – survival. A sense of purpose unites the conscious mind with components of the reflexes, both learnt and inherent, to integrate fully into the organism of achieving a common goal. But what drives us on to seek or improve? Psycho-biologist, Jaak Panksepp, may have found the answer with what he calls '*emotional operational systems*.' This theory will be discussed in the section on passion and drive.

> "I was magnificent, it was so simple, easy, I was just jogging. I understood Einstein's theory of relativity as time seemed to stand still. I could see everything before I did it. I felt so powerful, so in tune, in balance. It was a perfect melody, a rhythm, I was really flowing. The result didn't seem to matter. I knew I was going to win anyway. I was dangerous that day."

> Kris Akabusi 400M Hurdler.
> (1990 European Championships semi-finals on the back straight).

Zone Characteristic 4:
'Being in the moment,' focusing completely on the present. Unaware of time passing – a sense of time slowing down.

When we are not in The Zone we are either in a state of prolonged enforced concentration – a narrowing of awareness as we become preoccupied with the task in hand -or in a dreamlike state where attention drifts. In both states we become 'switched off' to our surroundings. An athlete in the heat of competition cannot afford to spend any time in a dreamlike state, only concentrating for short periods, as this will prevent him or her achieving the heightened sense of alertness necessary for a peak performance. There are also implications here for training or just working out, as I believe we cannot benefit fully from an activity if we are not appropriately engaged.

Fig 2.2 Michael Johnson and Maurice Green focused, poised and 'in the moment'.

So what does 'being in the moment' feel like? For me, it means being totally aware of yourself, your surroundings, and how you are interacting with your surroundings without these sensations becoming meaningless or a distraction.

If you are totally absorbed reading this book, and hopefully you will be, you may not be aware of other sensations. For instance, are you aware of what is supporting you at this moment? Whether you're standing, sitting or lying down there will be a surface beneath you providing support. If you are concentrating to the point of shutting out all else you are taken out of your immediate environment and transported elsewhere, much the same as being gripped by a good movie. You cannot be said to be in the moment if your mind is elsewhere.

On the other hand, if your eyes are just wandering across the text and not taking any of it in, you are performing an activity that is not engaging you fully. Again, you are elsewhere and not in the moment.

Somewhere in the middle, you can be conscious that you are reading a book, taking in what is being said whilst being aware of other sensations from your immediate environment such as the feel of the chair, sounds, and internal sensations like the movement of your ribcage as you breathe. Being in the moment, in my view, is when the senses can process and filter incoming signals without being overwhelmed – something often referred to as information overload.

So an athlete in The Zone is fully conscious of every action and its influence on the game, what that action implies, and how best to respond to it from moment to moment. The effect of their action is then fed back into this loop, assessed and responded to accordingly.

Practical

1 Scratch the end of your nose.

2 Now perform the same procedure but this time be aware of the movement of your arm as your finger comes into contact with the end of your nose.

You may have noticed a subtle difference in the experience of two similar actions. The first way is your habitual nose-scratching pattern performed without much conscious intention – it would be practically automatic if done in response to a real itch. In the second instance you are aware of the actual activity that has to take place in order to carry out your intention. You are consciously guiding and observing the action and therefore 'switched on' for the duration of the act, in contrast to the first instance where you only switch on once your finger has arrived at your nose. So for a brief time you are in the moment, existing in the 'real' world as you fully focus on what was happening and what was making it happen. It is also important to note that it doesn't require effort to do it the second way – just application.

This is a simple exercise to show the difference between an automatic reaction and mindful, conscious activity. Obviously to be in the moment whilst running a personal best is more fulfilling than scratching the end of you nose, but the principle remains the same. Being in the moment is a place we arrive at when we switch on, wake up and start living. Although athletes may use the term 'autopilot' to describe their visits to The Zone, I see this as a sense of the action being automatic while ultimately they are still in control of the decision-making process. Later in this book we shall look at simple activities to appreciate the subtle changes required to bring us into 'the moment'.

Stepping out of time

I have mentioned previously how we may have a different experience of time passing due to increases in information being processed. But one thing has always puzzled me about this aspect of The Zone. If on the one hand we experience time as slowing down, why on the other hand does thirty minutes feel like ten? If time appears to slow down then wouldn't time also drag? We say things such as 'time flies when you are having fun' or conversely, we watch the minute hand crawl around the clock when we're stuck in a dull meeting.

On one particular run I experienced being in The Zone, and had no idea that I had been running for well over ninety minutes. I thought I had been out for less than half that time. Perhaps changes in brain chemistry and consequent processing abilities once we have entered The Zone, explain a sense of being in the moment as we become aware of actions that are usually filtered out.

For example when I can run and be in the moment, a step is no longer just a step; it becomes many distinct phases of an action merging into one. I sense my lower leg recoil from my contact with the ground; my heel comes up towards my pelvis as my knee and hip joints flex; my lower leg then descends to the ground to start the process again. I am not doing anything different. But in place of experiencing a 'step,' it becomes a chain of discrete actions and therefore I experience a sense of more happening in a single phase – time slowing down. Add several thousand steps experienced in this manner together, and the accumulative effect is I become less aware of time as I become more alert to the moment. When I am absorbed, engaged and enjoying the activity, time no longer matters. If you are running in this state then your race time is likely to be good regardless of whether you are concerned about it or not.

Although I am conscious of more actions in each step it paradoxically becomes easier and simpler, as I let myself be aware – but do not allow any interference on my part. If everything is working well and going to plan, leave it alone!

> *"When I'm driving at my peak I appear to have more time to think as things happen in slow motion. I am better able to anticipate events and feel ahead of the other drivers. My vision 'expands' so I am totally alert to the positions of the other cars. I also become very much aware of every bump in the track and of my body as it moves with the car. In contrast, my poor performances occur when I feel I'm fighting the car, the track, the clock and my expectations."*
>
> Annabel Meade, racing driver.

Zone Characteristic 5:
A deep passion for the activity leading to higher levels of performance.

This experience provides further inspiration; it becomes self-perpetuating. In his book, Affective Neuroscience, Jaak Panksepp defines seven specific neural circuits and related behavioural patterns which he calls 'emotional operating systems.' He named each system depending on the type of behaviour the circuit promotes, such as LUST, CARE, RAGE, FEAR, SEEKING, PANIC AND PLAY. He sees SEEKING as vital for survival as it gives rise to curiosity, excitement and pursuit.

Its early evolutionary purpose was to drive the animal to search for food, shelter and a mate.

Activation of this system releases high levels of dopamine – the power switch that creates a state of heightened awareness, focus and arousal. The opposite state occurs when this system is inactive; we become de-motivated, tired and negative. Panksepp believes this system has to have a strong feel-good sensation or reward associated with the effort involved, to reinforce seeking behaviour. When the thought of a tough training session does not immediately arouse enthusiasm, what drives us to get going is that we know from experience we will feel better afterwards. So perhaps Panksepp's built-in SEEKING system provides a 'carrot and stick' mechanism encouraging us to take the steps along a path of self-discovery, driven by curiosity and the self-perpetuating reward of feeling good about ourselves when we achieve something worthwhile.

I believe this basic drive triggers Edelman's value system (mentioned earlier) to consolidate the active parts of the brain so they reinforce behaviour that ultimately ensures survival. Events that may interrupt training, such as an injury, break the reward-motivation-reward cycle. That makes it harder to return to a demanding schedule the longer we are out of action, causing intense frustration because we are not experiencing that high.

Zone Characteristic 6:
Sense of serenity – no anxiety, no ego so no worries about the outcome of action.

A study by David Collins, sports scientist and recently appointed Performance Director at UK Athletics, found that air pistol shooters achieved their best results when alpha wave activity increased in the left side of their brain prior to shooting. Alpha wave activity is associated with relaxed wakefulness, and is most prominent in the parts of the brain that provide an awareness of the body and its relationship with its surroundings. Other studies have linked alpha activity with improved accuracy in other sports such as golf and archery. These studies also found that only experienced players were capable of getting into the alpha state. Novice competitors were more likely to experience anxiety about their performance and could not achieve this relaxed, alert condition.

Collins' findings of increased alpha wave activity may explain the sense of serenity, but why would an athlete be in this relaxed state? Beta wave activity is the most common state for an active athlete as it is associated with a fully engaged mind focusing and interacting with the world outside. Alpha wave activity increases when we are relaxed and unfocused effectively putting the brain into 'neutral'.

There initially appears to be a paradox here. Surely the athlete in a beta state is better placed to compete? However, research into learning difficulties in children has found when in the alpha state, synchronisation between the centres of the brain improves, allowing for better processing of information. Perhaps those who are confident in their ability and have the relevant experience can pass through the beta (aroused) state into alpha (relaxed but still alert) state, because they are able to detach themselves from the mechanics of performing.

A number of athletes have described to me the sensation of taking a 'back seat' and feeling they are on 'autopilot.' If we are entering the alpha state our brains are better able to handle and process all the incoming data as synchronization is improved. Optimum integration is achieved at all levels and we experience a sense of inner stillness and immense satisfaction at our achievement. For me, this happens when the hedgerows are flying past but I have little sense of the effort involved in the act of running.

Perhaps this could explain why some athletes – who have spent most of their lives training and making sacrifices for their sport – when performing in front of millions at an important event, suddenly feel the outcome doesn't really matter once they're in The Zone. Does the experience of a peak performance mean more than the result of the race? Perhaps when we perform at our optimum we acknowledge there is nothing more we can do to win. Then there can be no reproach about the result and the performance itself becomes the reward, surpassing the importance of the result. The years of training pays us back as we feel a sense of total integration of mind, body and reflexes functioning as one.

Zone Characteristic 7:
No sense of effort. The activity becomes easy. Getting out of the way.

I believe this provides a significant clue to what is happening when we are in The Zone. Initially it seems odd that an athlete performing at his or her peak should describe such a sensation. Coe's record-breaking run (mentioned earlier) is a good example. On that occasion he felt he could have run faster and wasn't even tired after the race.

To begin to understand what may be happening here, we need to look at how we measure effort. When we say something is easy or hard work what do we base this judgement on? How do we sense effort?

When we wish to lift an arm, most of what happens is below a conscious level as patterns of muscle actions are selected to carry out the move. This is known as a conscious or voluntary movement, that is, we chose to move an arm in response to the wish to do something. We also have what is known as non-voluntary movement, initiated by a reflex without the need for conscious intervention on our behalf.

For example, if we tread on a nail the pain receptors in our foot send a message through the nerve into the spinal cord. A circuit, or reflex arc, is activated causing muscles to contract to pull our foot away from the source of pain. The same process happens if we inadvertently touch something hot. A spinal reflex is quicker to act, simply because the signals do not have to travel all the way up to the brain for processing and back again before a response can happen. We are not conscious of making a decision to lift our foot off the nail but are aware of the movement and the pain after the action has happened. The same sensation happens when the patella (knee) reflex is tested. We can see and feel the lower leg moving but have no sense of effort because we did not initiate the movement consciously. The signals for the muscles to contract came from the spinal cord, so the sensory information relating to the work done goes back to this level – hence the term 'feedback loop'. Therefore we have no sensation of effort, only the movement.

This set-up is similar to the command structure in a large organisation. The manager who gives the order wants to know what happens, but there would be no point sending a report to higher levels of management who know nothing of the order the manager has given.

Learnt patterns, also known as conditioned reflexes, are held in lower centres of the brain for quick access and execution. For example, we can drive a car making quick calculations for complex manoeuvres whilst still holding a conversation with a passenger. We are able to do this because the time we spend driving has laid down patterns of behaviour in centres of the brain that can be accessed with little conscious effort. The same applies to everyday activities such as walking, running and hitting a ball. An athlete who spends years training has all the patterns for their sport held at the same level, and often uses the term 'reflex reaction' when referring to a particularly good moment during play.

Could this explain why a vigorous activity can suddenly seem effortless? A number of athletes I have spoken to feel that when they 'get out of the way' performing becomes easier and they do feel lighter. On a bad day when everything feels so much harder, our sense of effort is greater because we may be using the 'wrong kind of effort' as we try too hard. This generally involves tightening the neck, shoulder and back muscles in a way that adds nothing to the movement. If we have consciously applied the effort, the feedback comes back up to the level from where it originated, that is, a conscious level where we will be well aware of the effort involved.

Practical

1 Stand and hold two books, one in each hand. Hold them with your fingertips with the spine facing down.

2 Be aware of the contact you have with the fingertips on the book.

3 Soften your jaw, neck, shoulders, arms and palms of the hands and allow your grip to loosen.

4 See how much tension you can release from your grip whilst still suspending the books.

5 Now let one hand at a time release so you drop the book.

How much tension could you release and still find it was sufficient to keep the book in your hand? Was the initial amount of effort you thought necessary well in excess of the actual requirement for the task?

"I was so surprised. Then again, I was so relaxed in the water, it felt amazing."

Pieter van den Hoogenband, swimmer,
on winning the gold medal at the Sydney 2000 Olympics.

Conclusion

I believe The Zone is a primitive ability and therefore an automatic function triggered by circumstances. It's a place we arrive at when we let go and allow it to happen. We cannot get there directly by deliberately trying, any more than we can get to sleep quicker by shutting our eyes tighter. If we are concerned about getting there we introduce an element of effort that I believe is the opposite of what is required. Even elite athletes often experience The Zone by 'accident' – they didn't deliberately try to get there. One moment they are performing, the next it's just happening.

A physiological description of what happens when we lift an arm appears complicated when all the electrical, chemical and mechanical processes are considered. In reality we don't need to know any of this because we just lift our arm. The complexities of The Zone are therefore in its definition. To enter it is far easier if we keep it simple and learn to get out of the way. The challenge of sport provides the means for our in-built 'survival' mechanisms to kick in and take us there – if we let it happen. What we feel in The Zone is our organism operating at its optimum, with every part of our body performing its function to full capacity; our thought processes call up the most appropriate learnt skill pattern aided by our inbuilt coordination reflexes. All components of the movement are fully integrated, working as nature intended.

Training methods that aim to improve specific skills and sensations associated with The Zone are, I believe, misguided. Whilst they may lead to some improvements, they will not deliver a true Zone performance. This approach can see only the destination and ignores the journey required to take us there. For example, it is not necessary to train in order to improve how quickly we can shift attention from one thing to another, because the ability is already there. Playing your sport with the right approach will help to sharpen these abilities. Smiling is associated with happiness; but it would be madness to strengthen the facial muscles used to smile in order to become more content. I believe we all have the ability to switch on and perform – we just have to learn to allow the process to work.

Whilst it is interesting to know a little about The Zone on an intellectual level it's really not much use if it remains theoretical. On a practical level we need to know what is not going to make it happen? The next chapter looks at the sort of habits that will keep you out of The Zone. If it's an automatic capacity then maybe we are doing something that prevents us entering it. Instead of looking at what we think we need to do, let's look at what we should stop doing to allow ourselves to slip in to The Zone.

3 What's Stopping You Reaching The Zone?

Morpheus: "How did I beat you?"

Neo: "You're too fast"

Morpheus: "Do you believe that my being stronger or faster has anything to do with muscles in this place? What are you waiting for? You are faster than this. Don't think you are … know you are."

(The Matrix. Warner Brothers Studios)

A sports coach told me a fascinating story about her young daughter's experience at a swimming gala. On the last length of her race she was some distance in front when suddenly she stopped. Her coach was in despair because she was obviously in The Zone, swimming the race of her life. Following the race, when asked why she had given up when she was clearly going to win, she replied that something had felt wrong because she could no longer feel the water. In fact, she was swimming so well that she was gliding through rather than fighting the water around her, a sensation top swimmers experience. Because this new sensation felt so wrong when compared to her usual experience, she had stopped. Had she relied on what she could see, that she was way out in front, and not what she was feeling, she would have won her race and learnt a useful lesson.

Here is another one. On my drive to work I used to see an elderly gentleman walking his dog. He first caught my attention because in spite of his age (probably around eighty years old) he moved with a wonderful free-flowing action and always had a smile on his face. Day by day I observed his effortless style and we soon began to acknowledge one another with a polite wave. Here was a man in The Zone. He could enjoy being in the moment during his daily activity.

Several weeks later I noticed a change in his gait. In place of his usual stride was a contrived march accompanied by a fixed facial expression and stiffness throughout his body. Thinking he might be in pain, I stopped to ask if he needed any help. Once I got closer the reason for the change became obvious. It was not physical but one of attitude; today he was wearing a tracksuit. He informed me that his doctor had suggested he took up exercise to maintain fitness in his later years.

So instead of enjoying his morning walk he was now 'working out' to keep fit. It was apparent that his idea of exercise involved making a natural activity harder, to guarantee he would get some benefit from it. Yet the extra effort succeeded only in adding unnecessary tension to his frame and strain on the joints and perhaps in the long term changing his concept of what free movement feels like. In place of enjoying his morning stroll, whilst keeping fit in the process anyway, it had become a chore because it was now exercise. Was he still in The Zone? Would he be experiencing any of the seven Zone characteristics discussed in the previous chapter?

In vain I tried to convince him to return to his 'natural' style of walking; but who is going to take the advice from some stranger in a car who contradicts his doctor of many years' standing? After a few weeks of this new regime I no longer saw him, or his dog.

Your biggest hurdle to a Zone experience is an invisible one. That's not because it is hidden from view; in fact, you can't see it because you are too close to it. It's right in front of your nose, or to be accurate, behind your nose. In the above scene Neo was performing according to 'rules' – learnt from another world – that did not apply in his present situation. Nature has gifted us with an incredibly complex piece of kit capable of observing, learning, adapting and remembering skills and strategies for every situation you will find yourself in. But problems can arise when the coach and the pupil are one and the same, i.e. yourself. How do you know if what you have learnt to do is the most efficient way to do it? Is there an easier way? You do not have the luxury of being able to experience what Michael Johnson or Rodger Federer feel when they're performing. A bell doesn't suddenly ring if you get it wrong, but get it wrong often enough and it will start to feel right! You can only tell you if what you are doing is familiar or not.

Remember the arm-folding experiment in Chapter 1? Familiar feels right, unfamiliar feels wrong. There would have been a time when you didn't fold you arms and you learnt by watching others do it. The important point is that you will have learnt to fold them in a particular way with either left or right arm on the outside. If you have never folded them the other way around you will never choose to do it this way and probably it will never cross your mind that it could be done another way. Of course how you fold your arms is up to you and doesn't really matter how you do it, as I doubt it will ever become an Olympic event! But whichever way you do it first, you are likely to become stuck with it; it's your habit for life. Folding your arms in the same way continues to reinforce the feeling of right-ness, whilst creating the set of 'rules' for this pattern that you will always follow.

Now what about how you run, jump or lift an arm – your basic move-ments that provide the building blocks for every action you could ever possibly perform? Why should these actions be exempt from the 'rules' that apply to your arm-folding habit? Of course they are not. So how you kick a football will be done in a way that you have learnt to do and that feels right. There are many ways to swing your leg; but would you ever try these out? I am not talking about technique as any competent coach can teach technique. Here we are looking at the building blocks of movement that form your technique. These are the pieces that make up the jigsaw, such as how you lift the leg; bring you lower leg through; how the upper body responds to the movement and what you do with your head. Your technique is the veneer on top that can be changed; but how you choose to perform your new technique will still contain your own basic movements governed by the rules you have unknowingly developed, based on your experience. We rely totally on what we are feeling, allowing it to influence what we are doing.

So in effect we all create our own unique bubble to exist in, but we can't see it because we are in it. To the snowman inside his dome the weather never appears to change! If you've developed poor habits relating to movement, how would you know? Loss of form and injury are the most obvious symptoms; but how can you accurately identify the cause when the fault lies with the very equipment you would use to diagnose and correct it? Never performing to your full potential is a less obvious symptom, simply because if you haven't been there, how do you know if you are underachieving?

A top athlete will consistently achieve top performances, but even at this level they will all have experienced a performance that surpasses all others by a considerable distance. One common theme occurring in their accounts is that it 'came from nowhere', 'out of the blue' or they were 'surprised' by their achievements. If these reported instances are accidental or came from nowhere, can we assume they were not doing anything deliberate to achieve them? I could have used the word 'consciously' but as you will discover, what you think you are doing and what you are actually doing can be two very different things. Do these vastly superior performances happen when the athletes burst their bubble and experience a totally new way of performing? Once beyond the constraints of self-limiting habits, they are free to step out of the way and allow the process to happen. Is this why it can feel effortless?

You could expect small variations in performance – but surely not the wide chasm between a Zone moment and a truly dreadful display. If your car handled like a Ferrari one day and a dumper truck the next, you would take it to the garage for a check-up assuming something had gone wrong. So why the gap? What is the difference? When you last achieved a performance worthy of a story for the grandchildren in years to come, what did you do differently? Can you identify a specific action? Could you predict it was going to happen?

In the last chapter I speculate that maybe we can try too hard and interfere with what should be a natural process. Here we shall look at three fundamental factors that determine how we perform every action and ironically, how conventional methods of training may take you further away from The Zone. These factors are:

- **Concept**
- **Habit**
- **Conditioning**

Amongst them they create the bubble in which we exist. In the movie, The Matrix, Neo had spent all his life unknowingly living in an artificial world. He was not aware of this until he escaped from his pod and had another experience to compare it with. Although in reality it's not quite so dramatic, you still live and perform according to the feel and rules of your own self-contained matrix. Until you have a completely different sensation of movement, how do you make the comparison? You may be totally unaware of what you are really capable of until you can perform outside your own set of rules. Let's look in more detail at these factors that make up what I call The Matrix Triangle.

Concept:

Your concept in this respect is what you think needs to be done and how you think it can be achieved. Every time you move you use parts of your brain known as body maps. These maps represent your body within the brain and are used to construct the individual components of the movement into a complete action. In scientific terms this process is referred to as feedforward. To shoot a basketball into the hoop you would have an idea of how much effort is needed and the trajectory required. A novice would be aware of having to think it through whereas an experienced player would generally be unaware of the process. Our novice, though, would already have entries in his body map for limbs and body parts that would be used in learning a new skill.

However, your maps may not always be an accurate representation of your body. Scientists have found that these areas can become 'corrupted' by poor movement and over-training, resulting in the wrong muscles being activated to carry out a movement.

Habit:

The 'default' pattern for an automatic reaction, i.e., no conscious thought about how you do it; for example, kicking a football. You may think about where you are going to kick it but you will not need to think about how to kick it because you have done it countless times previously. This is known as **conditioned** reflexes. How you react in certain circumstances sets up patterns of behaviour. A positive result heightens the chance that you will react in that way again when faced with a similar situation.

On a physiological level, **habits** are strong connections in your brain that are strengthened each time you use them. The Chinese have a wonderful saying that sums this up; 'habits are cobwebs at first, cables at last!' This explains why it can be so difficult to change a habit. The strong connections are easily triggered by stimuli often before you are aware you have reacted.

Conditioning:

This involves the activities you do, and more importantly, how often and how you do them. For example, an exercise will build muscles depending not only on the movements of the exercise do but also how you execute each move and which muscles you use – this would differ for each individual. The more you do something, the better you become at doing it this way. Pavlov famously conditioned his dogs by ringing a bell just before feeding them. In a short time the dogs began to associate the sound of the bell with the imminent arrival of the food and would salivate in anticipation of their feast.

The three key factors are interdependent as one influences the others – see figure 3.1. This process is fundamental to how we move, think and perform. I have placed a fourth variable – attitude – at the centre of this, which will be discussed later. For now, let's just look at the three factors of **concept**, **habit** and **conditioning**.

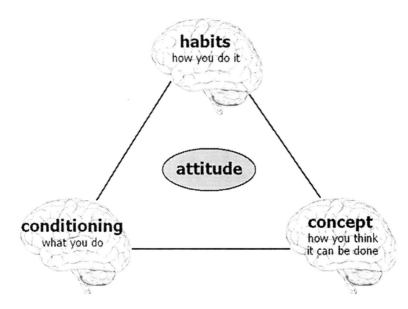

Fig 3.1 The Matrix Triangle. How you perform every single action is based upon how you have done it before. The amount of effort, how you move and even what you expect to feel are determined by the 'rules' you create.

Try the following experiment to see how the Matrix Triangle is influencing your movement. It is also interesting to watch others perform this everyday procedure to see what they do.

1 Sit on a chair and get ready to stand up.

2 Before you move, observe what preparations you want to make. Do you hold your breath? Do you push forward with the lower back and raise the chest? Do the muscles in your neck stiffen and pull back the head? Do you feel the need to push with your hands on your legs? Spend a little time to study this movement before continuing.

3 Get someone to watch you and feedback what they have seen.

Let's look at this from the viewpoint of the three factors mentioned earlier.

First, the **concept** you have of the movement determines how you will attempt to do it. This is likely to involve one or more of the actions in step 2. Your **concept** of what needs to be done is a result of how you have done it previously (**conditioning**). You will have found unconsciously a technique through trial and error that works when you need to get out of a chair. When you execute this technique your muscles are activated in a particular sequence associated with getting out of a chair, i.e., your **habit**.

From another point in the triangle, your automatic getting out of the chair sequence (**habit**) has helped to form your **concept** of the movement that leads you to do it using your muscles in a particular way time and time again (**conditioning**). That in turn will feedback into your **concept** and reinforce **habit**. For instance, if you do not use your leg muscles appropriately to get up you may start to use your arms to push yourself up. Repetition of doing it in this way may lead you to use your legs less and less and your arms more resulting in the **concept** that the legs are weak and cannot cope without the use of the arms.

Of course you will get out of all types of chairs in different circumstances whilst experiencing many different mindsets. It will not be exactly the same pattern executed every time, but your **concept** of how you move will result in the same actions being used to varying degrees every time because your muscles are **conditioned** for that type of activity.

If circumstances change – perhaps you have injured an ankle – the nature of this process should allow you adapt to the specific conditions. However, for a number of reasons to be considered later this may not always be the case. In fact the influence that **concept**, **habit** and **conditioning** have on you can become a liability. Your total, unquestionable reliance on and trust in this process will conceal any errors developing in the system. You may become aware of the result – that is, injury or loss of form – whereas the cause will not be so obvious. In fact, in many cases the effort people put into correcting a perceived problem only tends to reinforce the concept, habit and conditioning cycle because they do not step outside of their matrix. They then continue to use the offending concepts and patterns in a more vigorous way.

In the chair experiment I mentioned a number of preparatory actions that you may have made in order to get up, and I would bet my house that you would have done at least one. From the point of view of biomechanics (the study of movement, muscles and forces) the common preparatory actions in step 2 and the majority of any actions preceding movement reduce its efficiency, because they are unnecessary and simply waste effort. These inappropriate preparations work against the muscles trying to perform their function. Yet from my experience they are present in most adults when attempting to get out of a chair, regardless of athletic ability. Did you do any of the actions in step 2? Ask someone to observe you performing the experiment, and get him or her to look out for those actions as you may not be aware of what you actually do. Why do we do these extra preparations if they do not contribute anything to the movement? If you continue with the experiment you can begin to appreciate the force of the Matrix Triangle.

4   You are now going to try to stand up from the chair without doing what you have just noted (again it may be necessary to ask someone to observe your actions to give you feedback). How far can you execute the move before one, or all of the patterns from step 2 appear?

To execute step 4 successfully can be difficult. This is because these actions are part of your **habit** for 'getting out of a chair'; they're ready to go even before you start the action. The thought is enough to trigger the process. You would not attempt to start the move until the familiar conditions associated with the act – such as the sensation of muscle tension – are present. It is difficult but not impossible because although the **habit** exists, you still have a choice on how you react to the thought of getting up from the chair. But here lies the problem.

You do have the choice but how often do you exercise the option? When you next fold you arms or need to get out of the chair, see if you can stop, change the habitual reaction and do it differently. Why should you bother? How will that help your performance?

Learning to become aware of how you react is an invaluable skill for performance enhancement because it allows you to see where you may be habitually making things harder than they should be. (The chair experiment illustrates this.) It will also help you to make changes where required as you learn to take a step outside of your matrix. For instance, has a coach ever tried to change an aspect of your technique? It can be difficult, as what they are asking you to do will probably feel wrong – because it is not how you have learnt to do it. When you're trying to carry out their instructions your **habit** will be screaming at you that you can't possibly do it the new way because it doesn't feel right. Even if you know your coach is right, at the moment you come to do the new technique it is far easier to resort to your right-feeling habitual way, i.e. the strong cable connections in your brain as opposed to the gossamer threads that are yet to be put to use. If you find it difficult in training to let yourself do something different, it will be far harder in the heat of competition. After all, how can you possibly achieve any level of success doing it in a way that will feel wrong?

So what is the relevance of this to The Zone? If, whilst doing the chair experiment, you found you were doing too much work, and more importantly, you were not aware of it, how can you be sure that you are not using too much effort when training? Athletes in The Zone talk about the effortless nature of their performance. If you are applying the wrong kind of effort, could you be interfering with the reflex components of the action and therefore preventing efficient movement?

How you intend to do something and what you actually do to carry out that intention can be some distance apart. In the experiment above, did you plan to apply all that extra effort just to place your weight onto your feet and let the reflexes trigger the right muscles to take care of the movement? I believe more effort results in inefficient use, reducing the possibility of getting into The Zone. Sadly the emphasis in sport is invariably on physical exertion.

The 'effort is good' approach in my view is all too common in sport. There is nothing wrong with commitment and determination but if your effort is misapplied, all your hard work is wasted and potentially harmful.

Another factor that in my view can prevent us experiencing those Zone moments is – ironically – something most of us do to improve performance, and that is exercise. If you are currently experiencing injury or discomfort during physical activity, it is likely that you will be advised at some point to perform remedial exercises. If you are having difficulty with a technical aspect of your game there are usually practice drills to help you overcome it. If you're overweight it won't be long before someone recommends you take up or increase your level of activity that will invariably involve exercise of some sort. Tired all the time or depressed? Again, exercise will be mentioned somewhere on the road to recovery. Even if none of this applies we still feel the need to exercise to improve fitness and performance. The answer to all problems these days seems to be exercise; but does exercise do anything to address the causes of the above? Why and how do we get injured in the first place? Why do we struggle with technique? How do we get to be overweight and tired?

Exercise and attitude

Let's return to the story of the elderly gentleman on his morning stroll and look at this in relation to the Matrix Triangle. His concept of exercise had influenced his attitude towards how he was going to go about it. His attitude determined the application and overrode his usual free movement, to produce the stiff action he was using. He was now **conditioning** his stomach, back and muscles to tighten whilst doing his exercise which ironically resulted in restricting move-ment and breathing by increasing resistance. How long would it be before these actions crept into his habitual everyday walking style?

The mistake this gentleman made is not uncommon. I spent many years doing exactly the same and that is to apply the 'wrong kind of effort'. By this I mean work applied by the wrong muscle at the wrong time. Timing and efficiency are vital for good quality move-ment and if absent, poor performance and injury usually follow. Do you use the wrong kind of effort?

So this is how things can go wrong. If your attitude prevents you from being fully present in your activity because you are distracted by thoughts of getting a result, you may be unaware of small, seemingly insignificant actions creeping in. It doesn't take long for these actions to become part of your habitual patterns for that activity, effectively becoming hard-wired until you know of no other way.

For example, I've worked with many martial artists who actually make a backward movement prior to executing an attacking technique going forward. Speed is vital if you are going to score in martial arts and a backward movement not only slows you down but also signals your intention to the opponent. Then why do so many martial artists do it anyway? Invariably it is because the thought of the explosive nature of the move causes the artist to get set, or wind up before releasing his or her energy. It's a sort of breath in before going for broke.

Bruce Lee demonstrated the perfect technique in *Enter The Dragon*. Even using frame-by-frame DVD technology you will not see any preparation for the attack in his first bout of the film.

Attitude to the activity determines how you set about your approach. This is particularly noticeable with exercise. What do I mean by the term exercise? I define any activity done purely with the objective of achieving a pre-determined result as 'exercise'. In my view this approach deprives us of the real benefits to be gained from participating in an activity. What does the term 'exercise' mean to you? When I ask people this question the usual responses are – effort, repetition, a way to get fit, change shape, relieve stress or even escape from the real world! Exercise is something we set time aside for; we go to a specific place, get changed and then do some form of activity totally removed from any other sort of activity we would normally do, including our own sport. Afterwards we shower, get changed back into our ordinary clothes and return to our everyday activities. Many of today's well-equipped gymnasiums have TV screens visible from most places in the room so you can take your mind off exercise. Some people read books or listen to music when on the bikes – anything to prevent boredom and give the mind something more worthy to think about whilst the body gets a workout.

Compare this sort of activity with going to the swimming pool as a child. I always looked upon that as a real treat and would spend well over an hour leaping, jumping, swimming, diving and playing games with my friends. How many muscles did I use then? Did my cardio-vascular system get a good work out? What skills did I learn and improve upon? Was it fun? It sure was! Did I go swimming to get fit or change my shape? Was any of that on my mind when I was having the time of my life? Absolutely not! When does the thrill of a trip to the swimming pool, or any other activity, become a chore? When we start to think of it as exercise. Yet we do not lose this thrill for action. Take a bat and ball and a few friends to the park and all of the above can be achieved and then some. To be consciously absorbed in an enjoyable activity with a bit of competition thrown in, will challenge all your faculties and encourage the sort of integration of your total self in a way nature intended.

But what about the working of those specific muscles that can only be done with a machine at the gym? Chuck Wolf, director of sports science for the U.S.A. Triathlon National Training Centre in Florida acknowledges this problem with the exercise machine saying,

> *"… our love of machines has caused us to lose sight of the way the body functions. Machines are ideal for multiple repetitions of the same movement patterns along a single plane. Unfortunately, that's not how we move."*

I would like to stress that there is nothing wrong with exercising as such, especially if you find it enjoyable. It is not the activity at fault; it's the attitude and state of mind that is important. A trip to the gym can be beneficial if you are mindful of what you are doing and whether you are using your body as well as nature intended. For instance, do you need to tighten your neck and make a face when doing a bicep curl? What are you doing with your lower back when working on your quadriceps? If you can be aware of your whole self when using specialist gym equipment you will either use it more to your benefit, or decide that there really is no point in strengthening your piriformis muscle all by itself.

Sadly, the dominance of 'exercise culture' in today's sport and fitness world can take the joy of movement and spontaneity out of activity that was present in our youth. The strict discipline of an exercise regime can make us forget the very reason why we once enjoyed sport and activity. Young children love to run and jump. This free-play is vital for developing their sense of balance and reflexes. When we are young we do not need to know this. We play because it is fun and feels good.

I believe the regimented and repetitive nature of exercise can actually reduce our range and freedom of movement by promoting a level of control and tension that is counter to how our bodies work. We do not have the direct physical connections from the conscious, thinking part of our brain to the muscle at the end of the chain and therefore are unable to control individual muscles. Muscles work in groups, sometimes aiding the movement, sometimes resisting the move-ment to protect muscles and joints and at other times stabilising the structure. It's a complex business and well beyond our capacity to determine exactly which muscles need to do what at which specific time to bring about a movement. Exercises that focus on specific muscular activity for precise execution contradicts the hierarchy and command structure of our nervous system. It places control at a higher level in the brain than necessary and in my view overrides our natural coordination reflexes. We simply do not have the knowledge at this level to even contemplate doing it. It is comparable to asking the managing director to sweep the factory floor. I believe it is pos-sible to confuse our system by too much attention being given to the control of a movement.

Remember the centipede –
  A centipede was happy and quiet until a toad in fun,
  Asked "Pray, which leg comes after which?",
  This set his mind in such a pitch,
  He lay distracted in a ditch,
  Thinking how to run.   (Anon)

The body knows only of movements and not the individual muscle actions that are involved, any attempts to control muscles directly will, I believe, keep you out of The Zone.

It Ain't What You Do …

Attitude is a central factor in how you do your exercise, and for that matter in all your activities. Do you move in the same manner when you are walking to work on a cold, wet Monday morning as you do walking to the beach on the first day of your holiday? In the case of exercise, the mere thought of it can give us the attitude that it will be hard work, otherwise it won't be beneficial. When I ran purely for fitness in the belief it would help my karate, I didn't feel I was worthwhile unless the run had been a tough one. This approach led me to lift my shoulders and tighten my back in order to get a good work out.

Although the 'no pain, no gain' message of the 1980s appears to have been discredited, its ethos lives on. One example is power walking (not to be confused with the sport of Olympic walking.) What should be an easy, natural activity has been transformed into a 'formal exercise' by creating a technique that increases the amount of effort required. The belief is that walking in this manner will use more calories and increase cardio-vascular fitness without the need to run. Its supporters claim it is less likely to lead to injury than running, but I would argue that the advice given for power walking can only result in setting up a number of bad habits and misconceptions.

1. *Keep your head up, back straight and body aligned.* How would you follow this advice? I see people tightening their backs and fixing their posture. How do you know if your back is straight? If you knew how to align your body it would already be aligned!

2. *Stride out, but don't lengthen your stride so much that your knees lock, which can lead to injury.* Any attempt to stride out will land your foot in front of your body and increases the stress on your knees (see fig 3.2.) Whether you're running or walking your feet should land under your body and head.

3. *While walking with hand weights or weighted gloves.* What does walking with weights added to your arms or legs do to your body dynamics? How does it change your normal walking or other activities? You will build muscles to be used in a way that is not your natural movement. You can even buy weighted vests!

4. *Pump your arms.* This action is generally done with the shoulders raised adding tension to the neck.

Do you need to do any of these actions to walk? Are they going to aid free, natural movement? On the contrary, they are most likely to interfere with breathing, movement of the joints and the action of reflexes that would coordinate the activity for you. Could you get into The Zone and experience the effortless nature of walking by doing the power bit? I admire the commitment of the many people I see power walking whilst I'm out running but I firmly belief they would be far better – and still keep fit – either running or just going for a 'natural' enjoyable walk.

Earlier I defined exercise as any activity done purely with the objective of achieving a pre-determined result. In the last chapter we looked at Csikszentmihalyi's four specific criteria that he states need to be present to enable a Zone moment. Briefly these are a challenging activity; you have the skills to meet that challenge; there are clear goals; and you can easily monitor your performance. Obviously all of these can be present in an exercise routine as well as a sport, but remember we can only enter The Zone if we are absorbed by the activity. Can we be said to be totally absorbed if our mind is elsewhere when we're exercising? If I watch MTV whilst I'm on the treadmill, how can I possibly get into the moment and enjoy running for the sake of running?

Fig 3.2 Power walking. Note the position of the foot in relation to the body and line of impact through the knee and hip. This will cause undue stress to all the leg joints and right the way up her spine. Also check the raised shoulders and head position, pulled back, as a result of pumping the arms. Ironically, this sort of photo is used to promote the virtues of physical activity!

Upsetting the Balance

If the sensations experienced in The Zone are what it feels like for every part of our body to be working at its optimum, then all our training should work towards this. Many of today's popular methods in my view do not encourage what I think of as total body integration. Muscle isolation training, core strengthening and postural exercises are some of the main culprits that ignore some of the basic principles of human movement and therefore are likely to obstruct your path to The Zone.

Remember your body knows only of movements, not individual muscle activity. When you bend your arm you think of the movement and not of contracting the bicep. You do not have direct connections from the conscious, thinking part of the brain leading to the muscle. When you think you are giving the right commands, how can you be sure that the muscles you wish to control are responding?

One study looked at subjects sitting on a Swiss ball (a large inflatable ball.) When instructed to use their core muscles to balance, the subjects were found to be using more activity in the muscles of the limbs – the body's built-in way to maintain equilibrium. When questioned, none of the subjects was aware of this. There is a gap between what you ask the body to do and what actually happens. We shall look at the implications in the next chapter.

REALITY CHECK

If you want to use this sort of training ask yourself the following questions before commencing with an exercise,

1   Am I capable of individually and directly controlling certain muscles to move? Remember there are no direct connections from your conscious part of the brain to the muscle at the end of the chain.

2   How can I be sure that what I feel when I do something with a muscle is actual feedback coming from that muscle. There is no way of knowing that what you feel is actually coming from the muscle you are attempting to control.

3   Do I know enough about how my body works to successfully coordinate myself? Can I do it better than my natural reflexes?

4   How will the movements I am performing help with my sport or fitness? Would I use my muscles like this in the course of my usual activities?

Did nature intend us consciously to control individual muscles to keep us upright and moving? Is that repeated anywhere else in nature? If muscle isolation exercises are intended to strengthen weakness, we have to ask why are these muscles weak? I would argue again that it's due to inappropriate learnt habits that are preventing our bodies from coordinating themselves. This involves muscles not being activated at the right time or conversely, being too active when they should be relaxed.

Conclusion

I believe that continued use of such techniques, creates the habit of applying excessive muscular effort and control in areas where they are not required. Consequently this will interfere with the naturally coordinated and efficient movement associated with being in The Zone. To use the old cliché, the whole person needs to be considered when addressing the issue of fitness for whatever sport you play. To address this fully we need to go higher up the command structure, past the muscle, and even past the lower parts of the brain that contain the movement patterns. We need to go to the top of the organism, to the bit that does the thinking, and assess what you are asking your body to do. Your body does exactly what you tell it to do. The issue is, do you know exactly what you are telling it to do?

4 Beyond The Matrix

In the previous chapter we looked at how it is possible to create your own matrix – your unique set of rules that ultimately establishes the limits of your performance. You can't see it because you exist within it. Yet there are moments when you may have experienced a performance so different from (not to mention easier than) anything else you have ever achieved, that you find it hard to describe your experience. As we have seen, these Zone episodes happen when you can get out of the way and temporarily step outside your matrix. The old rules don't apply and suddenly your movement, decision-making and sporting skills escalate way beyond your expectations.

The objective of this chapter is to show you how you can use the Matrix theory in a way that will change your concept of your body and how it performs. We shall look at:

- **Habits and their impact on movement and performance**
- **Using the 'wrong kind of effort'**
- **The advantages of 'being in the moment'**

This will help you gain an understanding that will help you experiment with movement in a radically different way.

We will start with the basics and build upon these skills to use later in the book for more demanding activities. From my own experience and through working with others I have found most people are unaware of the basics of movement. When you consider how heavily we, as sports people, depend on our bodies and the demands we put upon them, this comes as quite a surprise. But perhaps if we consider the sort of conditioning sports people endure it is not such a mystery.

Right at the start of our sporting life we are encouraged to work hard to achieve success – but then we're left to our own devices about how exactly to go about it. We are taught and accept that anything worth achieving requires effort. The message that 'if effort is good, more effort is even better' is evident in the majority of sports. But what kind of effort are we talking about? What did our sports coach mean when he said we had to try harder? Do we add a little tension to our bodies to impress the coach? Perhaps if I look like I'm really trying I'll make the team.

The same principle applied in school. So long as you looked as if you were concentrating it was possible to gaze out of the window, daydream and get away with it. All you had to do was screw the face up a little to look deep in thought, contemplating today's lesson. If the action taken achieves the desired result the behaviour is reinforced regardless of the method. I am convinced that things said to us in our formative years by those we respect such as parents, teachers (well, some of them) and sports coaches, leave little seeds that remain buried deep and influence us in imperceptible ways throughout our lives. How old were you when you realised it was safe to pull a face even if the wind was likely to change direction?

Even when we come to think differently, these seeds have long since influenced behaviour that develops deep-seated habits. The 'effort is good' seed is probably still influencing your concept of movement today. Behavioural therapies recognise childhood experiences as a pivotal factor in an adult's psychological health, so why not his or her physical health also? A youngster desperate to make the team will assume the coach knows best and put away childish thoughts of sport being about free-flowing movement, excitement, and above all great fun. Conventional thinking has us believe that commitment is demonstrated by effort, sacrifice and perhaps even the odd sporting injury early on to confirm your determination for success. We must not forget the importance of role models, either, when it comes to influencing behaviour. A child imitates the actions of their sporting heroes on the field who invariably sell the same 'effort is good' message.

So I return to the question – what kind of effort? When you say you are going to try harder, what does this mean? How are you going to apply yourself in a situation where you are going to try harder? Do you concentrate on the task differently? Remember the way you learnt to concentrate in class and the facial expression associated with it. Do you use your facial muscles more when you try harder? A little later in this chapter we shall look at the implications of muscle activity in the face and neck area, in relation to your movement. When you want to run faster what do you do? It's obvious you have to move your legs faster but how do you go about it? What actually happens?

It's common to see even professional athletes apply the wrong kind of effort to run faster. The runner leading the race on the last bend senses a fast approaching competitor and in an effort to increase speed, ends up putting on the brake. The head goes back, the shoulders come up and he appears to run on the spot as the second placed athlete flies past. Do you lift your shoulders or tighten your face and neck to make the legs go faster? I did.

Evolve don't revolve!

How you move is a process you probably devote little attention to, because usually you will be concentrating on what you need to do rather than how you do it. What do I mean by this? The chair experiment is a good example. When the telephone rings you concentrate on getting to it so you can answer before they hang up. You probably wouldn't be conscious of how you are getting out of the chair and how you are walking to the telephone. Why should you? It sounds like a lot of wasted effort. Yet until you can develop an awareness of yourself in action, you will remain trapped within your performance-limiting matrix guided subconsciously by your concept of what it should feel like. Keep doing the same things and you will get the same results. So you have to go into the unknown, take a step outside of your matrix and prevent yourself from going around in circles.

The 'being in the moment' and 'totally focused on the present' experience of athletes in The Zone can be experienced in everyday life. Skills learnt outside of your training can be beneficial in your sport, just as your sports training can help your business and personal development. Yes, it does require effort to drag yourself into the present; but it's a different kind of effort. It's about focus, not concentration. Some would describe it as a sort of detachment.

The effort involved is in the application of awareness to the present task in hand and being in control of your decisions. For example, if you are in The Zone sitting in your chair and the telephone rings, you would not immediately jump up to answer it (bells and conditioned reflexes again!) In The Zone you could consciously decide whether to pick it up. If you decided to answer it, you would then be aware of how you moved up from your chair using no inappropriate effort, and be aware of yourself walking toward the telephone. When you get there your arm would move effortlessly to pick up the receiver (absent of any tension because it doesn't require much effort to lift it.) All of this would not take any longer than your habitual way; but your sense of time would be different because you are experiencing the present and not reaching out for the telephone in your mind before you get there.

Of course you could make a decision to not answer it and do nothing. Does this seem a little dull or complicated way to answer the phone? Transfer this sensation of 'being in the moment' to a sporting situation, however, and it's sublime. To be living in the present or the here and now can be extremely rewarding. Remember Csikszentmihalyi's criteria for experiencing The Zone says nothing about the task needing to be exciting – just challenging. You may say that answering the telephone is hardly challenging and I would agree if it were done in our more usual distracted state; but to do it consciously is a challenge!

Being In The Moment

So what are the benefits of being in the moment? Being in the moment gives you freedom of choice over how you respond, and prevents stereotyped habitual reactions. It allows you to think clearly, assess the situation and make the right decision; often with the sensation that you have longer to make your mind up.

> *"When your scull is being held in place on the starting pontoon there is a strong combination of excitement and fear of the unknown, it's a risk. You don't want to be catching a crab (get the angle of the blade wrong in the water). I had something to prove that day and asked myself to dig deep. I was seeing the race before it started and knew it was going to be big about half way through. This was where I had to make my training count. At 1000m (half way) it was between me and two other boats. At 1500m one of them dropped off and it was just me and the other guy. I started to pull away and said to myself that I would gain 6 inches with every stroke. I increased my rate, it was starting to burn but I knew I could sustain it. I felt I was up for it that day and had something to prove to my coach. The Saturday before the race I hadn't performed well and she had ripped into me. Today I needed to show her something and felt I had proved my point."*
>
> Joel Grant-Jones, rower.

You are conditioned by what you do and how often you do it. If your first reaction to getting out of the chair is to tighten your lower back, it becomes part of that pattern and you are no longer aware that you do it. Every time you need to get up from a chair the lower back muscles automatically tighten, and you would not consider moving until you felt this tension that gives you the go ahead for the movement to start.

So why does this matter? Such preparations are not mechanically efficient as they add nothing to the movement and in most cases restrict it. In addition to tightening the lower back, most people pull the head back and are totally unaware that this is happening even when it's brought to their attention. The muscles at the base of the skull, known as the sub-occipital group, are the most sensitive in the human body. Sensitivity is measured by the number of muscle spindles per gram. The sub-occipitals (220+) contain over four times more than the next most sensitive muscle group in the body, the quadriceps (around 50). Muscle spindles are activated when the muscle lengthens thus triggering the stretch reflex that contracts the muscle, to prevent damage. The muscles of the neck are hugely influential in coordinating muscular activity throughout the whole body and work in relation to the inner ear balance mechanisms. When you are not in the moment you are more likely to use your inefficient muscle habits to move. Being in the moment appears to change everything and release these inappropriate habits, hence the sense of effortlessness.

If your first reaction to moving includes pulling back your head these highly sensitive muscles slacken and therefore become dormant, so failing to trigger the appropriate reflexes responses that would aid your movement. Part of your body is now working against another, preventing the total integration required for a Zone performance. If these highly sensitive muscles at the base of the skull are slackened because the outer muscles of the neck and shoulders have tightened and pulled the head back, they are feeding 'false' information about the direction you are travelling towards. Nature has evolved so that movement is directed by the head leading and the body following. Think of a shark, gliding through the sea, that can rapidly change direction to catch its prey in its jaws; a cheetah, sprinting across grasslands, whose body appears to be steered by its head as it tracks the movements of its lunch. If you inappropriately contract the neck and shoulders muscles and pull back your head, even if only by a fraction, will your body still want to move forward? Or does it think a backwards roll is coming?

Humans may be on two legs but movement is still coordinated primarily by reflexes triggered by neck and shoulder muscles. If you tell your body one thing, i.e., "I'm getting up", but your actions tell it something, for instance, "I'm pulling my head back therefore I'm going to roll back", then you have a mismatch. Your conscious decision will win but it will cost more effort than required. When you are in the moment, as in a Zone experience, you are conscious of the decision making process and able to select effectively how you respond – including not tightening the neck and shoulders.

If The Zone represents a moment when every part of you is working together without interference (getting out of the way) then this is what you have to practise. From what I see I would say the majority of us have developed many habits that prevent us from getting out of the way. At the same time these habits have corrupted our 'body-sense.' The mechanics have gone wrong, resulting in shoulders lifting when just the arms are needed, the pelvis twisting when the legs move and many muscles contracting for movements when they really should be releasing – torn hamstrings being an obvious example of the consequences.

Don't Just Do It ...

Let's try some experiments with thought and action. They will appear quite simple and pedestrian for a seasoned athlete such as yourself, but please stay with me on these early procedures. I am not trying to teach you how to move your head or lift a leg but to practice being aware and fully present in an activity, or 'being completely involved in an activity for its own sake' – an essential requirement for The Zone.

The objective of the following activities is to play with movement and it's important to do this with an open, enquiring mind. These are not exercises as they are not to be done with the goal of achieving a specific result. The purpose of an experiment is to be objective and not subjective. You should not try to predict the outcome of the action, which in this instance is how it will feel. What you think it should feel like, to move a leg for example, is based on your existing concepts and there is little point performing these with your old habits.

In all the activities in this book I would like you to think of movement as a release, or letting go, to allow the movement to happen. For example, if you hold your arm out in front of you and let go it will drop back to your side. Obviously in this case it is the gravitational pull that brings the arm down but in all movement, gravity and momentum play a role. In many phases of a movement it's a matter of letting go to allow part of the body to complete its action. These procedures will help you appreciate where you can let this happen to prevent unnecessary effort.

Patrick MacDonald, an Alexander Teacher trained by F.M. Alexander, defined the two forces at play in a gravitational field and their impact on the human body. He called these Force A, the pull down causing a heavy feel in the body and, Force B, the push back up or an anti-gravity force that produces a lightness in the body. You may notice how different you feel on one day when your sport is easy when compared to another when it's hard going. The difference is usually one of lightness on the good days, heaviness on the bad.

When your body moves in a coordinated way using gravity to its advantage, it capitalises on Force B. When running you bounce off the road with a spring in your step. Your responses are sharp and you feel able to change direction quickly, with poise, on the tennis court or sports field. Maybe your golf swing is perfectly timed as you maintain balance. Lightness is not the first adjective that comes to mind when describing those great performances, but it's what leads to the effortless sensation more commonly reported by athletes in The Zone.

The first of the experiments in this chapter will look at an area that is vital for total coordination; the head and neck.

Activity: *The Nodding Donkey*

We will start with a very simple movement from a joint most people are unaware of, despite its importance to body movement as a whole. The joint in question is the atlanto-occipital joint and is situated where the skull sits on the spine. I say that most are unaware of its location because when asked, the majority will suggest a point somewhere lower down and further back from its true position. Try it. Ask as many people as you like and see just how far their guesses differ. People will point to where they probably move their heads from and will have therefore built up an inaccurate picture of their own body. This picture (the body map) is used every time we move. If the picture is suspect, the subsequent movement will be. You can't put your finger on this joint because it is in the centre of the skull.

1 To get an idea of its position, place both index fingers in the groove behind your ears and appreciate that the joint is roughly in between your two fingers and almost level with your eyes.

2 Leaving your fingers there for the moment, look up and think of the movement from this joint between your fingers.

3 Then look down, again with the thought of the pivot point and allowing the movement from here.

4 How did you do? Now try using less effort. Think of your eyes leading the head to look up whilst allowing your head to tilt back on the pivot point like a seesaw.

5 Release your head forward by letting go of the back at the neck and your head will drop back down without your having to pull the head forward. Your head is heavier in front of the pivot point of the atlanto-occipital, and if the muscles at the back are released gravity will do the rest.

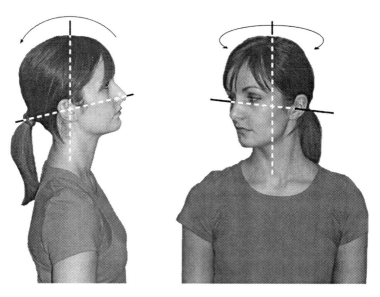

Fig 4.1 The location of the atlanto-occipital joint (where your head sits on your spine) is higher and further forward than most people would guess. Your concept of where this vital joint is situated will influence how you move your head and consequently will have a big impact on all your movement.

Now, move your head from side to side, again allowing your eyes to lead the head. You should be able to do this without the shoulders moving. The objective is to get the head moving with the absolute minimum amount of effort enabling you to experience movement in a different way. It is worth checking that you have not tightened the jaw, as this will interfere with the neck and shoulder muscles. To soften the jaw, allow the teeth to part a little whilst keeping the lips lightly together. Now the next time the ball is moving to your right, see if you can turn toward the action in the same manner. This is the challenge. Can you be in the moment and be able to turn your head with minimal effort without the shoulders twisting or lifting?

I have included this head and neck procedure early on due to the influence the neck muscles have on movement. This area can act as your brake. If it's tight your brake is on and will restrict all movement to a degree. If you can keep it free and allow the head to balance on top of the spine, then the brake is off and movement becomes freer and lighter.

After a number of Alexander Technique lessons I began to realise my brake was on most of the time. As my sensitivity increased I realised it was still on when previously I had thought I was taking it off. The problem with tight muscles is that they are less sensitive, because the spindles are not stretched and therefore feed less information back to the nervous system that is directing your muscle activity.

Movements of the head trigger activity in the body below. Even before birth, movements of the head activate primitive reflex responses to get the limbs moving, encouraging the development of the connections from the brain to the muscle. From about six months of age the reflexes that will see us through life begin to appear. These are the reflexes that enable us to hold our heads up and coordinate controlled total body movements.

Activity: *Standing Order*

The next activity is something you will probably do frequently and unconsciously, and that is standing. As activities go it's not that exciting, is it? However it is possible to use these moments to sharpen your skills of awareness and observation.

In this experiment you are going to appreciate what gravity can do for you. Gravity gets a lot of bad press and is usually blamed for many of our ills including poor posture, muscles aches and pains, because humans stand on two legs instead of four like most other creatures on the planet. We use terms such as feeling down, the wind taken out of our sails or we feel deflated when things are not going too well. These are associated with collapse and losing the battle against gravity. Yet if you learn to become aware of the energy you can generate from the floor, it opens up a whole new area for exploring movement.

1 Stand with your feet about hip-width apart.

2 Imagine you are being pulled into the ground by a weight attached to the end of your spine.

3 Now picture a light shining out of the top of your head and notice the difference compared to 2.

4 Move the source of the light to your centre, about four centimetres below your navel. In martial arts this area is known as the hara and is thought to be the source of our vital energy. Let this light flow out through your legs to the floor, along your arms, up your spine and through the top of your head. You can also think of 'growing from your centre'.

5 Keep this thought of light flowing from your centre and think that it could support you.

6 Take a few paces forward whilst you continue with no 5.

(See Fig. 4.2 overleaf)

Fig. 4.2 The slump (A), attention (B) and poised (C) standing positions require very different muscular activity to maintain an upright position. The poised (C) stance uses the least amount of effort. I have placed a line down from the location of the atlanto-occipital joint (where your head sits on top of your spine). Notice where the line passes down the body. In (C) the weight of the head passes directly down the spine and through to floor requiring less muscle activity to maintain balance. Check which one most closely represents your standing posture – to get the right answer, ask your partner!

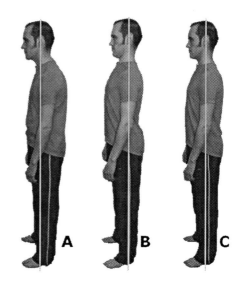

A B C

Activity: *The Poker Face*

1 Is your jaw clenched?

2 Allow your teeth to part a little but leave the lips lightly touching. The muscles holding the mouth closed are active even when we are not talking, as they prevent the jaw from dropping open due to the pull of gravity.

3 Check your eyes are not fixed. Allow them to 'soften' and let the light bounce off this page into them.

It's a common habit to stare and fix the eyes when running or focusing on something happening in your sport. Remember that eyes don't work like search beams. Light comes into your eyes allowing them to act like windows, albeit with a focusing ability, but the seeing is done by numerous locations in the brain. You don't have to grab the image off this page to read it, because the image arrives at the back of your head without your having to do anything to help it other than keep your eyes open. Attention is a slightly different matter, because you are not always aware of what you are seeing. So whilst reading this section just think of softening your face and eyes and let your head sit on top of your spine.

The next time you are exerting yourself in training, just check to see what you are doing with your facial muscles. Do you need to do this? Could it interfere with your movement? I did an experiment by running hard to see how long it was before I felt the urge to pull a face. When it happened I then tried to see if I could carry on running without doing it. It was possible and it did feel a little easier once I ceased to contort my face. In addition to using up energy with nothing to show for it, it also tightens the neck muscles and consequently puts your brake on.

Perhaps also, the action of pulling a face feeds back and encourages the idea that what you are doing is hard work. Do athletes in The Zone pull faces? The facial muscles are very sensitive and any activity in this area would probably prevent an athlete describing his or her performance as effortless. A martial artist is taught to keep a 'soft face' when sparring not only to prevent giving away his intentions to his opponent, but also to keep his poise. Top sprinters are well aware of tension in the face having an adverse effect on their speed, so when they run you will see their jaws move.

© Getty Images

Fig 4.3 The Canadian team at the World Rowing Championship Banyoles 2004. This is the start and the most explosive part of the race as the crew looks to get off the blocks into a good position. Check the expressions of their faces. Why does the rower on the right look so comfortable? Do the faces being pulled by the first three crew members help?

Please Release Me ...

In a moment we will take the lessons of the previous activities and apply them to taking a step forward. You are going to perform this activity whilst being aware of your face, head, neck and shoulder muscles and the floor under your feet. This may seem a little unusual because obviously to take a step involves a leg. This is where you are going to start to think of movement in a wider sense. To perform any movement there are

- muscles that do the movement by moving bones

- muscles that restrict excessive movement at the active joint, to prevent injury

- muscles that stabilise the frame so we don't fall over

- muscles that have to release to let the movement happen

This last category tends to get overlooked simply because the muscles concerned don't appear to do anything directly for the action. Yet their role is just as important, because in their relaxed state they allow the movement to happen - as well as remaining sensitive to changes in position to feed information back constantly to the nervous system. An example would be the neck and shoulder muscles in the act of getting up from a chair. From a biomechanical viewpoint they are not required but as you may have discovered in the earlier experiment they could be contracting when performing the activity.

Activity: *One Small Step*

The objective with this procedure is to practise a simple movement without getting ready to carry it out. On the surface this looks just a little too easy for someone who takes his or her sport seriously. It's just a step, for goodness' sake! However, you may be surprised how difficult it is in practice to perform this simple, everyday action consciously and in the moment. Let's just remind ourselves that the objective is to do this action a different way.

1 Stand with your feet below your hip joints and let your arms rest by your side.

2 Think of taking a step forward but do not start to move. Observe what you want to do to get ready to step forward. Do you lean to one side? Are you starting to fall forward or hold your breath?

3 Now think about light coming from your centre and flowing along your arms, up your spine and through the top of your head as in the previous activity.

4 Keep this thought going and release your knee forward away from your hip; imagine falling up as you step forward.

This is about appropriate timing and minimal effort. To take a step forward you have to release and allow the movement to start with only the slightest effort to let the knee bend and lift. It's like a car on a hill releasing its brake.

Fig 4.4 Think of a thread pulling your knee forward and let your lower swing through like a pendulum once your foot has come off the floor.

Conclusion

These procedures can help to identify some common causes of making movement harder than it needs to be by adding unnecessary actions of your own. I see many sports people who expend a huge amount of effort on actions that not only are totally wasted - because they add nothing to the movement - but also are actually working against them. They are completely oblivious to it. The reason for this is partly habit; that is, it's an automatic reaction and therefore they are not conscious of it. It's also partly because there is a gap between what you intend to do and what actually happens.

If the picture in your mind of your body (your body map) is inaccurate, then this adds a further complication. For example, to perform a golf swing you need to know what you have to do to make it all happen. Right from the start this could be questionable if your map of your arms includes the shoulders, e.g. using your shoulders to hold a book when it can be done adequately with just the hands and forearms. Are your shoulders raised now? If yes, were you aware of it prior to my question? A golfer gripping the club using her shoulders will get in the way of the rotation of the torso and prevent the free flowing action required for a good swing. The more she does it like this the better she will get at doing it like this, until the tension in the shoulders and torso becomes part of the swing pattern. She is not doing it purposely because on an intellectual level she will know it's not going to help. Once at this point she will not attempt to start her swing until she has 'prepared' herself in the way that feels right. Any good golfer can tell you that you do not need to try and hit the ball hard as any added effort is going to interfere with your movement. The weight of the club will produce its own momentum and the golfer needs to let it go and just make sure it hits the ball. This is done prior to the swing by getting your position right. If she does become conscious of the shoulders being raised, she may then do the opposite and try to pull them down whilst leaving tension elsewhere. This will lead to a tug of war between the muscles involved and further restrict movement.

To manage the gap between your intention and the outcome successfully, you will have to become conscious of the moment. That means to live in the moment; the here and now; *to become com-pletely absorbed in the activity for its own sake.* When you can do this you are in the Zone and everything becomes easier as things begin to take care of themselves.

5 Getting Back to The Zone

You are reading this book because you would like to get into The Zone more often. Once experienced, it's something you just have to rediscover because little compares to the 'high' of performing at your peak. The good news is that if you have the determination and are willing to experiment there is no reason why you should not become a regular 'zoner'. The better news is that you can get there by relearning a skill you had naturally as a child. This skill is knowing how to 'be in the moment'. It sounds simple, but sadly many lose this ability and spend most of their waking hours being everywhere else but in the moment. When we are in the car we are thinking of our destination and what we are going to do when we get there. In the office we are thinking about what we might do later. Even when participating in our sport, inappropriately placed attention will be taking us out of the moment.

Mindful participation in an activity can be thoroughly rewarding; even seemingly mundane tasks can take on a new meaning. The objective of this chapter is to develop your skills of focus and awareness, to help bring you into the moment. Once you can master and apply this skill it will open up a whole new dimension to your training. The procedures here also have an element of re-education with regard to your body and movement. Training out of The Zone leads to a diminished body-sense as you will unconsciously use your habitual patterns that may or may not be efficient, as some of the previous experiments have shown. These habitual patterns invariably contain unnecessary muscular actions that prevent free-flowing movement.

Repetition of these actions causes us to lose sense of what free movement feels like or how much effort is required to move our arms and legs, and so on. Quiet, mindful activities will help the re-education process and eventually the lessons you learn here can be taken into the more physical activities of your sport.

When I was a business analyst in the telecommunications industry, one of the techniques we used for finding solutions to procedural problems was to reverse the process and deliberately design a solution that would fail miserably. Surprisingly, many of the ideas coming from this technique were found to be disturbingly close to current practice.

The traditional approach to training is the system I believe you would design to deliberately keep you out of The Zone. The emphasis is in the wrong place, physically and psychologically, with the importance placed on achieving results whilst leaving you to guess how to attain them – and without necessarily having the relevant knowledge to go about it. The experiments in this book already may have demonstrated the limitations of your body-sense and difficulties you face when trying to do anything outside of your dominant habitual ways.

The Zone Test 1

The crucial first step to getting into The Zone is to become absorbed in the activity. Csikszentmihalyi described it as *being completely involved in an activity for its own sake* – **but how you define the activity is fundamental to starting the process**. Ironically, the emphasis on getting a result will prevent you from achieving this vital first stage. Let's look at the example of a training run and apply Csikszentmihalyi's four criteria necessary for the chain reaction of brain processes that will take you into The Zone, to demonstrate what I mean. These are:

1 **the presence of a challenging activity** – for this example we will use a six-mile run.

2 **the perception that your skills match the challenge** – I have trained well and feel the goal is a reasonable one.

3 **clear goals** – let's say I want to do it in under 42 minutes.

4 **the availability of instant feedback concerning your performance** – I can check my stopwatch at each mile.

I may be a little anxious about being able to do the run within my target time. It would be a disaster if I fail because if I think it's achievable, what would it mean if I couldn't do it? Have I been doing the right training? I would start my run in a determined manner because I'm motivated and fired up and totally focused on my performance, i.e., my running speed and time at the mile stages. Because I'm motivated I set my mind to it and focus on the road ahead.

At the first mile I glance at the time and I'm pleased because it's ahead of my target and I contemplate setting a personal best. Encouraged by the time I have 'gained' I press on and see if I can shave a few more seconds off the next mile. At the next mile I look at my watch but find I've lost the extra seconds gained earlier. Although I'm still on target I'm concerned that I have no time to play with. At the third mile I'm disappointed because I'm now outside the required time and will not accomplish my goal unless I speed up. I push on and now keep a close eye on the time in between the mile stages. I start to feel a little better as I'm well into my stride and the speed picks up. I push harder as the last mile comes into view; it's hurting but my pace is still good and there is not far to go. I'm now keeping one eye on my watch as the lamppost marking the finish is rapidly approaching, and I am on course for a personal best. The last few strides cause some pain as I strain every sinew to dip past the post three seconds under my target. That is what you call a race against the clock and I beat it! Exhausted, aching but elated at the personal best, I head for a shower.

A young athlete once asked her coach how would she know if she was in The Zone, to which he replied 'don't worry, you will know'. Here we will be a little more exact and use the characteristics from the second chapter. For this to qualify as a Zone run I would have experienced the same sensations as athletes describe in their peak moments.

Let's just recap on what I would have to experience. I would have:

- been totally absorbed and focused on the activity
- experienced an inner clarity and understood exactly what was required to complete it
- had a sense of ecstasy and being outside everyday reality
- been completely focused on the present and unaware of time passing
- been inspired by the experience
- had a sense of serenity, no anxiety, no ego so consequently no fear about my performance
- had no sense of effort

Could my run achieving a new personal best be considered a 'Zone run'? I was certainly *totally absorbed and focused on the activity*, or was I? What was the activity? Easy, it was running for a personal best, but I was not focused and totally absorbed on *running* as such because I was pre-occupied with the time. My focus was on the stop-watch and my speed, but not on the actual act of running.

Did I *experience an inner clarity and understand exactly what is required to complete it*? I suppose the answer would be yes. At each stage I could check my time and re-assess how I was going to complete the task. Although you could argue that my understanding of the requirements to complete it, that is, run faster, may not have been that clear. How did I go about running faster? Were my efforts to run faster as successful as they could have been? Perhaps I tightened my back or lifted my shoulders when trying to run faster, a common habit in runners; but I wouldn't have necessarily noticed because I was focused on my stopwatch. I would have felt the extra effort and assumed this effort was directly helping me go faster.

Perhaps I had *a sense of ecstasy* when I knew I was ahead of my target, but I'm not sure if there was a sense of *being outside everyday reality*. Striving to get something completed on time and within a tight schedule sounds very much like everyday reality! Perhaps I can get a tick in the box for *being completely focused on the present*. Well actually no; it was hard to be focused on the present when I was thinking of where the next mile marker was and if I was on target to get there in time. I was always somewhere further on and not thinking of where I was at that moment. I was also painfully *aware of the time passing*!

I was definitely *inspired by the experience*, surely? Well, was I inspired by the experience of the run itself or the achievement? As I stood in the shower afterwards, what was the most memorable thing I took from the run? The joy of the run, or the fact that my time was three seconds inside forty-two minutes? If the run had taken six seconds longer and I had failed my target, would I have still enjoyed the experience? It's obvious I did not have a *sense of serenity, no anxiety, no ego so consequently no fear about my performance* and certainly could not have boasted there was *no sense of effort*.

I may not have got many ticks in boxes to qualify it for a Zone run but at least I got my new personal best! So apart from knowing I can run six miles in under forty-two minutes what else did I learn from the run? Well, perhaps not that much that would be useful for my next run. What if I had started to experience some discomfort during the run? Could I apply my knowledge gained from my previous outings?

Let's look at this run from a different angle.

1. **the presence of a challenging activity** – a six-mile run as before.

2. **the perception that your skills match the challenge** – I have trained well and feel the goal is a reasonable one.

3. **clear goals** – here is the difference. My goals are now to be in the moment to maintain awareness of my running style and enjoy the run!

4. **the availability of instant feedback concerning your performance** – I can check my neck, shoulder and back muscles are relaxed; my legs are kept free from tension and I can allow my feet to rebound

up from the road (a more detailed explanation of efficient running technique is in Chapter 7, Running in The Zone).

In this case the activity remains the same but the emphasis is now placed on how I go about running – not how quickly. In place of monitoring my speed and time, I am going to focus on areas where I may be making it harder than it should be and see if I can prevent unnecessary effort. It is easy to believe that effort is good and will help you to run faster, so surely more effort is better? Yet many actions initiated by the thought of picking up the pace are wasted and may even slow you down.

I set off and for the first mile contemplate what makes me run faster, and how I can maintain that speed for a lengthy period. Obviously my legs have to swing faster but I cannot afford to waste energy doing that, so it comes down to efficiency and style – getting the most out of each stride with minimal effort. So if I can maintain my awareness on the how I'm applying myself to the act of running to ensure maximum efficiency – that is, remove the inappropriate effort – I will increase my speed in the process. I could choose to check my time at the mile markers, but it should not change directly how I am running. For instance, if I maintained my focus for the first mile and the time is good, I'm somewhere on the right track. If the time is poor, my focus will have been in the wrong place and it is this that has to change.

I become Sherlock Holmes and look for clues where I may be making the run harder than it should be. I can use the second mile to experiment with my level of focus and open it up to take in the scenery whilst still maintaining an awareness of myself running in my surroundings. Before I approach the second mile I could guess whether the time will be good. Is my estimate based on how much effort I think I have applied? On occasions when I've thought I had run a good time, it can turn out to be slower than I anticipated because the effort I have sensed may have been wasted – such as lifting my shoulders, which would have slowed me down. At other times an enjoyable, relaxing run can be turn out to have a fast time. Remember the experience of Sebastian Coe and his world record 800m!

I am now really enjoying being totally absorbed in an activity on a pleasant evening and do not even look at the stopwatch at the three or four mile stage because I don't care what it says. I know I'm going fast because the hedgerows are flowing past, there are no aches or pains and as I approach the fifth mile my curiosity gets the upper hand and I take a look at the time. It's good and I tell myself not to alter a thing due to the time. I don't need to try to run faster, just to maintain my awareness of any tension that may have crept in unnoticed. I find I have lifted my shoulders a fraction and allow them to release again. As I finish I stop the watch but don't look at it for some minutes because it doesn't matter. I have achieved my goal by remaining conscious of the act of running throughout the run and have enjoyed the experience. Later when I do check the time it's 41:54, three seconds faster than the previous run.

The Zone Test 2

Let's apply The Zone test again. With this new approach I certainly was *totally absorbed and focused on the activity*. The activity was running; I maintained a focus on the actual act of running and where I was running throughout the six miles. Because I achieved my new goal of maintaining awareness of my running style and reducing unnecessary effort, I could *experience an inner clarity and understanding of what is required*. How? The requirement was to run efficiently, not fast. With experience I know which actions are not efficient and as long as I can prevent these happening, I can improve the ratio of energy used to distance covered. I believe the inner clarity comes from quietening down the activity in my body. Less effort equals fewer muscle contractions equals fewer signals travelling around it. I am better placed to listen to my body.

I did experience a sense of ecstasy but this time it was not due to the time. On this occasion it was a response to doing something I enjoy and doing it well. There were no distractions. I was able to watch the tractors in the fields, listen to the birds overhead and be wary of approaching cars. However they did not prevent me from maintaining an awareness of myself running through the countryside, because they were part of the activity. As I was absorbed in the activity and *in the moment*, my mind didn't drift off to unrelated subjects so I stayed *focused on the present*, an *experience outside my usual everyday reality*. I didn't have to be aware of the time as it wasn't the goal for this run.

The further I got into run the more I became *inspired by the experience* as my confidence soared that I was capable of achieving my goal. The experience has also fired my passion for running and provides the motivation of going out and repeating the whole thing. *A sense of serenity, no anxiety, no ego so consequently no fear about performance* was evident early on and stayed with me to the end. I had very *little sense of effort* and paradoxically, although I was maintaining awareness on the activity I felt I was *getting out of the way*. Why should this happen? It is important to differentiate between thinking and doing. When I talk about maintaining awareness of my neck and shoulders for example, it's a thought process, taking a back seat in a detached non-judgemental way. It is not something I have to do. Obviously I didn't really have to check all the boxes on my return to see if I was in The Zone, because I already knew!

So in addition to Csikszentmihalyi's four criteria being present, it is the goal you set that can determine your attitude and whether you enter The Zone or not. The goal you have in mind will influence not only what you set out to do, but more importantly, *how* you set out to do it.

Would it have been possible to get into The Zone using the first approach? After all, sports people achieve it when setting out deliberately to get a good time and win. The answer is yes, but it would remain much more a hit or miss affair to get into The Zone in this way. Remember, for most athletes it comes as a surprise. On the occasions they do get there by the 'old' method; perhaps for some reason they suddenly let go and enter into the moment and the natural flow follows from there. It isn't deliberate on their behalf, hence the surprise.

The difference here is we are looking to enter The Zone consciously, by allowing ourselves to become absorbed in the *true* activity. When we can master this skill, the natural flow from there will be into The Zone as the process of heightening our awareness through total integration and synchronisation comes into force. It doesn't happen for me every time yet, because I am still developing the necessary skills with the knowledge it will be an ongoing process. However, my times in The Zone are far more frequent than they were with my traditional approach to training – the 'no pain no gain' school of physical activity.

Prepare for The Zone

So from a practical point of view, what is the best way to ensure you are in the right mindset to get into the moment and into The Zone? Dr Patrick J. Cohn, a sports psychologist, believes you can create a mindset that will increase your chances. His research identified five keys to entering it.

1   **Are you confident?** Few athletes can perform well if they lack confidence on the day. Self-confidence comes from a belief in your ability and technique. Past performances, success and properly targeted training regimes help to build confidence and the knowledge that you are up to the challenges ahead. We shall look at confidence in Chapter 8.

2   **Can you become immersed in the task?** This involves knowing what to focus on and how to refocus when distracted. This also means staying with the present task in hand and not getting ahead of yourself. It is therefore important to determine what is relevant to your sporting performance and develop abilities to focus on these cues.

3   **Can you let go of your mistakes?** Mistakes are going to happen in sport but they have to be put behind you immediately. Holding onto the guilt is only going to have an impact on your next move. Cohn recommends having a plan for 'releasing bad plays'.

4   **Does it feel automatic?** Practice can help to develop skills that feel automatic and effortless – 'a strong memory pattern of a skill'. This can allow you to focus on your strategy or your opponent,

if the activity can look after itself. Some describe it as being 'on autopilot' although I dislike this term as it suggests no thought is involved.

5 **Do you stay in control?** Being in control of your performance as well as your emotions. Stress levels must be controlled in a way that allows you to perform at a higher level of arousal, but not to the point of anxiety or fear that would impede functioning. Pressure can be used to focus on the challenges.

This is the *before* and you will see how being in the moment can play its part in all five of these points. For now, if we return to the *after* we are in The Zone, i.e., the seven Zone characteristics, and look for some connection, can we match cause to the effect? Do they all come at once? From my early encounters I would have said yes. However now I feel there is an order, but once the first one occurs the rest are experienced very quickly and probably simultaneously. Below I have arranged the seven Zone characteristics into some sort of order. I would also say that I define *feel a passion for the activity* as relating to the moment you are in The Zone and not in the sense that you have a general passion for your sport. Obviously you need to have an interest in your training otherwise you would not devote so much time to it.

Firstly, **you have to be 'in the moment'** (1) before you can become **absorbed and focused on the activity** (2.) Then you will experience **an inner clarity, have a sense of ecstasy, feel a passion for the activity, have a sense of serenity, no worries about performance** and **have no sense of effort** (3,4,5,6 & 7).

You may think 1 and 2 are the same but there is an important difference. You cannot become *absorbed and focused on an activity* if you are not *in the moment*. Being in the moment will also allow you to choose *which* activity you are going to focus upon. **Remember, if you are concerned about the result or outcome of something that has yet to happen, you are not in the moment**.

Dr Cohn mentions confidence as a prerequisite; if you are anxious about your performance you will also struggle to get into the moment.

In common with Csikszentmihalyi, all five of Dr Cohn's entry criteria require an element of being in the moment. Confidence can be lost if you are ahead of yourself and are concerned by the outcome to the point of distraction. We've spoken about being in the moment before you can become immersed in your activity. Cohn's suggestion for having a plan for 'releasing bad play' is an excellent strategy. If you dwell on a mistake, it will obviously affect what you are going to do next and your confidence is lost. You are no longer in the moment and the process is halted. As for a plan, if you can drag yourself into the present and accept what's done is done, it will not influence your next play. The automatic, effortless sensation comes from a state of letting your body's support and movement reflexes work. Staying in control and not letting the situation get to you is again about being aware of how you are reacting to events around you. We shall discuss how to use the stress of performing to your advantage later in the book.

Above all else I see the capacity to *be in the moment* as the most important attribute for a successful athlete, or in any field for that matter. Every other skill can be developed from this as the starting point. To be fully present in whatever activity you are undertaking allows you the opportunity to respond appropriately in all situations. Being in the moment is a vital, yet rare skill, but from our point of view, is the entry point to The Zone. So as I see it, all you have to do is to focus on the present and there you are – in The Zone! Sounds quite simple – but how do you actually go about achieving it consistently in practice? Also when you are in the moment, what do you focus upon?

Get real!

It's time for some activities to appreciate what being in the moment entails, and to experience what is really happening when you sharpen and focus your awareness. The activities involving movement are best done with a partner who can read the instructions and observe how you perform. You can then exchange places and see the activity from an observer's point of view. Both roles are learning opportunities. If this is not possible you can either use mirrors, or connect a video up to a monitor so you can observe in real time.

These are not exercises because they are not done with a specific objective to build fitness in the conventional sense. We are looking to develop fitness in its wider context and that is an ability to observe, think and act in the most efficient and appropriate way for the current situation. Your performance is not related purely to your level of fitness (in the conventional sense). A formula one racing car still needs a driver who knows how to handle it and when to make his move.

Think of these as experiments. An experiment is done to test a theory and learn something about what makes things happen. Correct procedure for experimentation states you must not pre-empt the outcome, so please don't try to get them right. Remember what you think is right is decided by your habits. The theory we are testing is that we can get into the moment by focusing our awareness on the true activity. For instance, running is not the activity; movement of your limbs is the activity. As soon as you think of running, you bring into play your habitual running pattern and drift out of the moment as you pay little attention to the actual act.

Before we begin the procedures, I want to emphasize the importance of how you carry out the instructions. When asked to 'think,' check that you are not 'doing'. For example, if you are asked to think about standing tall this should not involve tightening your lower back and pushing your chest out. This is doing and not thinking. As soon as you attempt to 'do' a thought, you will probably engage unnecessary muscular activity based on what you believe to be the right way to do it – your habit. Of course if you knew how to stand tall you would be already standing tall. To think but not to do is a skill that requires training because we rarely achieve it. What exactly does this mean?

"… but what I like doing best is Nothing." said Christopher Robin,

"How do you do Nothing?" asked Pooh, after he had wondered for a long time.

"Well, it's when people call out at you just as you're going off to do it, 'What are you going to do, Christopher Robin?' and you say 'Oh, nothing,' and then you go and do it."

"Oh, I see," said Pooh.

"This is a nothing sort of thing that we're doing now."

"Oh, I see," said Pooh again.

"It means just going along, listening to all the things you can't hear, and not bothering."

"Oh!" said Pooh.

Activity: *Just being*

the challenging activity – to sit and observe all around you but not to react to what you sense

the perception that your skills match the challenge – you could do it as a child, just like Christopher Robin

clear goals – to be in the moment

the availability of instant feedback concerning your performance – if an unrelated thought pops into your head you are not in the moment

1   Without moving, become aware of whatever is supporting you and anything else you are making contact with whilst reading this book.

2   Sense the clothes on your body, the movement of your ribs, the sights and sounds about you.

3   Observe all this information but do not allow yourself to react to it. For instance, you don't have to move to feel the contact with your clothes or appreciate the support of the chair or floor.

4   Allow yourself to hear the sounds about you but do not try to make sense of them.

5   Be aware of your eyes moving across this page whilst still taking in everything else.

6   In a moment you can put this book down and sit for a few minutes to sit and think – but not to do. Keep your eyes moving and let the light bounce off the objects in front and enter your head. Do not try to interpret what you see.

7   Check your jaw isn't tight – allow a slight gap between your teeth but keep your lips lightly touching. Just sit, not do. Try it now …

How did it go? If you were able to practise this detached thinking for a few moments you will have experienced being in the moment, focused on the present but also having a sense of being outside everyday reality – ring any bells? We spend the majority of our time reacting, whether we are aware of it or not, to events about us. Habits become hardwired and are triggered without us even noticing. These will include some of the common habits covered earlier, such as getting set in preparation to move. In these situations the conscious mind is by-passed, effectively switching off our ability to think before we act. You may argue that habits speed up reaction times and yes they do – but only if we are conscious of the moment.

You probably have experienced what is known as a 'reflex reaction' when your response was lightening fast and accurate, but you will have been aware of events leading up to these moment of glory. Contrast that experience, with when you were taken completely by surprise or caught napping. You have to be conscious of the moment before an appropriate learnt subconscious reaction can occur, i.e., a sporting skill. Other subconscious reactions, such as the withdrawal reflex, are active even when we are not. If you stick a pin in the toe of a sleeping subject she will still react. Yet an experienced boxer can be caught completely unprepared by the sucker punch, if he were not focused on the present.

We will continue with the activity most beneficial to performance – breathing. However, this is not a breathing exercise. You are not going to focus on trying to take a deep breath to force unnecessary oxygen into the lungs; if your body needed it you would already be breathing faster and deeper.

Activity: *Breathe Easy*

the challenging activity – to observe yourself breathing without trying to control it

the perception that your skills match the challenge – you have breathed since the day you were born

clear goals – to be in the moment

the availability of instant feedback concerning your performance – you will be able to feel the movement of your ribs and soon become aware if you are trying to move them yourself. You can sit, stand or lie down to do this procedure.

1 You can do this standing, sitting or lying down. To get into the moment you are going to focus on the activity but you are not to think of breathing as the activity.

2 Be aware of the movement of air in and out of your nose.

3 Notice the movement of your ribs as your lungs expand and deflate.

4 For a few moments just let yourself be 'breathed', take a back seat and observe where the ribs are moving. Note: there should be no pause between the inhalation and exhalation phase, because this is a symptom of interfering with the free-flow of air.

5 Let your mouth drop open slowly and exhale, adding a slight whisper to it.

6 When you reach the point where the flow starts to dip (do not empty your lungs!) close your mouth and do absolutely nothing.

7 The air should begin to flow back instantly in through your nose and push the ribs out and up slightly. You do not need to attempt to move your ribs as the incoming air will inflate your torso. If you try to move the ribs it will interfere with your natural coordination.

8 Return to just sitting and breathing and repeat the 'whisper breath' every few minutes. Listen to the sound of your breath – it should sound like a gas leak. Any unnecessary tension in the body will alter the sound.

I asked you to focus on the movements and not to think of this as breathing because breathing is not the activity. It is too tempting to try to do the breathing by sucking in air and pushing out the stomach as soon as we think about it.

If the ribs are not moving you are holding tension somewhere in your frame causing the muscles of the torso to act like a straight jacket. Your facial muscles and nose are not used to do the breathing; you do not need to suck in because air will flow in due to the lower pressure in your lungs. Your nose is the way in to your lungs and should remain passive in the breathing process.

Activity: *The chair challenge*

In the third chapter, we tried an experiment of getting up from a chair. This is an action you do many times a day but probably pay little attention to the act, as you will be thinking of why you are getting up. We will use this activity to begin the process of practising being in the moment.

the challenging activity – to get up from a chair consciously without 'getting set' by tightening the neck, shoulders or lower back

the perception that your skills match the challenge – you can get out of a chair and you have experience of being conscious

clear goals – maintain awareness of what you want to do to make your neck and back move and then not do it

the availability of instant feedback concerning your performance – if you don't have a partner to feedback you can use a two mirrors placed so you can see the movement from the side. Remember it has to be instant feedback, so video is not suitable unless you can wire it directly to a TV in front of you.

1   Sit on a chair, towards the front of it, and be aware of the support coming up from the chair through your pelvis and up your spine. Let that 'push' your head toward the ceiling. Be aware of your ribs moving as in the previous activity.

2 Think of your head leading your torso, including your pelvis, forward – but be careful not to stiffen the back. To move from the right place, think of a hinge at the level of the chair where your legs meet your pelvis.

3 As you move forward notice how the weight coming onto the feet tightens the muscles at the front of the leg. This is your positive support reflex getting ready to support your weight.

4 Now think of transferring the push from the chair to the floor and let your weight come over your feet.

5 Do not use your back, just think of yourself being light and 'fall upwards' over your feet, and let your legs straighten.

6 As you perform this be aware of the movement in your hips, knees and ankle joints and of your head being sent up toward the ceiling as your body straightens.

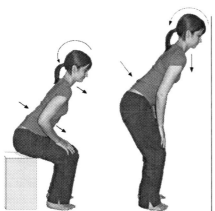 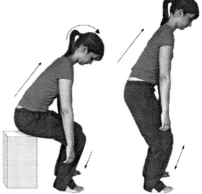

Fig 5.1 Common actions you will see when getting up from a chair include head being pulled back, shoulders lifted, chest pushed forward and lower back tightened – all completely unnecessary and make the movement harder than it should be.

Fig 5.2 It's a lot less effort if you just allow your weight to come on to your feet and let the push from the floor activate your leg muscles.

If you think of this movement as standing you will use your usual, habitual 'getting up from a chair' pattern and switch off as you perform the act – then switch on once you have arrived at your expected destination. To get into the moment you will have to focus in the present true activity of the intermediate stages, consisting of the movement in your joints and changes in weight distribution. When you can focus on what is really happening during the activity, you are in the moment and therefore on your way to The Zone.

Activity: *On the Ball*

the challenging activity – to catch or not to catch a ball consciously.

the perception that your skills match the challenge – you have the ability to make decisions and you can catch a ball.

clear goals – to practice being in the moment and experience that moment when you choose to act.

the availability of instant feedback concerning your performance – you will immediately know if you cheated and didn't make your decision in the moment.

This one is easier with a partner but if you don't have someone available this could be done using a wall and you can react to the rebound.

1 Stand or sit a short distance away from your partner. Your partner will toss the ball gently towards you and you will make the decision to catch or let it go as the ball is about to leave their hand.

2 If you decide that you are going to catch it be aware of the movement of your arms and hands to complete the act. If you have decided to leave the ball and not make an attempt to catch it, just watch the ball but do not allow yourself to make any movement.

3 Experiment with how late you can make the decision to catch or not to catch. If you are finding it difficult and you are moving when you've decided not to catch the ball, you are not in the moment. Stop and become aware of the floor or chair supporting you, your breathing, your facial muscles and movement of your ribs.

4 Do not lose awareness of your surroundings and focus entirely on the ball. It doesn't matter if you drop the ball; this is not the activity. The activity is whether you consciously can make a decision in the moment.

5 If you choose not to catch, observe whether you are still reacting by holding your breath or tightening any of your muscles.

6 Throw the ball back to your partner and observe how they react.

7 Talk to each other about what you have observed.

You may have learnt from this procedure that it is no use trying to jump into the moment at the instance your partner is about to throw, because you have already reacted. You have to be in the moment continuously and that includes when you bend down to pick up the ball.

Activity: *On the Ball (for real)*

the challenging activity – to balance on an exercise ball.

the perception that your skills match the challenge – you have the necessary reflexes to do it.

clear goals – to stay balanced on top of the ball without trying to balance yourself.

the availability of instant feedback concerning your performance – you will fall off!

If you haven't already got an exercise ball I recommend you buy one as they are very useful pieces of equipment, and are not expensive. You may have seen them used for doing all sorts of stomach exercises but I suggest the greatest benefit you will get with one is learning to balance on it.

1 Sit on the ball with your feet on the ground and spend a few minutes getting used to the position.

2 Now tilt forward a little from your hips and push back with your

feet so you roll onto the middle of the ball, and take your feet off the ground.

3 Let your arms rest lightly by your sides on the ball and keep your jaw relaxed by leaving a slight gap between your top and lower teeth.

4 See if you can relax, keep breathing and be aware of the small movements of your arms in response to any change in your position.

5 When you can keep a relaxed jaw, neck and shoulders, your head will naturally maintain a vertical position and help to activate the most appropriate muscles to keep you on the ball. – see fig 5.3 and 5.4.

6 When you are comfortable start to move around, but continue to stay relaxed and allow your body to adjust and coordinate itself.

7 If you start to roll back just tilt forward from your hips to keep your head over the centre of the ball.

Fig 5.3 and 5.4: you can see the head's righting reflexes working to balance her body. The head stays close to the vertical and the arms make 'automatic' movements to keep her centre of gravity over the top of the ball. It is important to remember that these reflex movements cannot be controlled by consciously trying to do it.

As you become more confident, increase your movements on the ball and allow your body to respond accordingly. Remember, any effort you make directly will be interfering and is more likely to lead to you falling off!

If you can stop yourself becoming tense in the neck and shoulders at the thought of losing balance, you will stand a much better chance of staying on the ball. As you move around your balance and coordination reflexes will work every muscle in your body to keep you in position.

To do this successfully you will need to do what I call 'getting out of the way' or in Alexander terms 'non-doing'. This is a route to getting into the moment and by now you will know what happens when you can achieve that. This procedure is not about learning to balance on a ball, because unless you are a circus act you will never need to do it. The purpose is to practise getting out of the way to allow your body to coordinate itself with minimal effort. You can apply this thinking to all your activities, including the most vigorous sport.

Conclusion

One of the elements that's key to the quality of your performance is being able to make decisions and act upon them quickly. Your fitness and skills count for little if you cannot make appropriate judgements based on what is happening around you. There is no point being the fittest player on the field if you cannot read the game. This raises the question of what is fitness? A tri-athlete places very different physical demands on her body compared to those of a golfer or tennis player. All have to be fit for their specific purposes. However there is one skill that's essential for success in all sports; the ability to assess the situation quickly and act accordingly.

Many athletes in The Zone describe having an age to think about what to do next and a sense of time slowing down. In Chapter 2 we looked at why this may be the case and you may have experienced this in some of the procedures here. For example, the experiment to scratch your nose will have shown that when done with an awareness of the movement of your arm, you had the opportunity to change its direction or stop the movement altogether. If you are not in the moment and habit determines your reaction, you do not have this luxury. For instance, a player who strikes out at an opponent in frustration cannot call back his fist once it's set on its way. When fully in the present all options remain open – even the option not to react. The main benefit of being in the moment is you have the ability to choose your response.

Before you start your next training session, do not set your goal to achieve a personal best or even to get into The Zone, because neither is the true activity you will need to become immersed in. Make your goal to maintain your awareness of how you are moving based on what you have learnt from the procedures practised so far. This is the indirect way to The Zone. Do not let your face change in order to focus; furrowed brows or fixed eyes are a learnt pattern for concentration but will do nothing to help your awareness.

> *"I knew that to beat Frank (Fredericks) I'd need to run a great curve, so as we wedged into the blocks, I concentrated on the curve, on the technical things I needed to do to get up and around the curve, to fling myself up out into the lead. But with the start, I made a tiny mistake, one of those sprinter's fractions. I was thinking so much about the curve – the second zone of the race – that I didn't think about the first. Instead of reacting to the gun, I waited and got left on the blocks."*
>
> Michael Johnson on the importance of being in the moment;
> he lost this 200m race to Frank Fredericks – a rare occurrence for Johnson.

When you are in actual competition, keep your goals the same. Focusing on trying to win is the same as going for a personal best – it's not the true activity. If you can maintain attention to yourself and how you are reacting to the run of play, a good performance will follow. Great if you win, but if you lose make sure you can find the reason why. We would naturally all like to be winners but that just is not possible on every occasion. Make your long-term goal that of improvement through developing a better understanding of yourself. Your sporting career, whether professional or amateur, will then be a rewarding one for many different reasons.

6 To Boldly Go …

Because you take your sport and training seriously you already will be committed to your fitness and performance enhancement. After all, what's the point in training if you are not going to progress? We can take a great deal of satisfaction from learning and improving a skill, as this is probably reinforcing our deepest primeval desires for survival. Seeing obvious signs of improvement also provides an incentive to continue. Few people will persist with a sport in which they see no chance of progressing their skills.

Performance can be measured in times, scores or distances; but there are other less tangible ways in which you may be improving. Absence of injury, consistent form and sustained confidence are all signs of moving in the right direction. I would also add that continued enjoyment of facing the challenges of your sport is a healthy sign of progression. If the thrill of participating has gone, it's likely you have stopped moving forward and it is difficult to improve without drastic changes. The challenges of enhancing your performance should not have to include overcoming the boredom of training. If they do, you are going wrong somewhere and I doubt whether you will be getting much benefit from your sport - and you're likely to achieve diminishing returns.

Likewise, you must not allow yourself to plateau by resting on your laurels. World-class athletes are at the top because they never stop looking to develop their ability. When Michael Johnson won gold in the 200 metres at the 1996 Atlanta Olympic games it was described as the perfect race, whereas Johnson himself knew he had stumbled on the third step off his blocks. He was not going to let the victory overshadow the need to find out why it had happened. For someone like Johnson, a tiny, almost unperceivable error could lose him a few hundredths of a second that may be the difference between gold and silver.

At any level, performance enhancement may be achieved by the smallest of adjustments to your action. The experiments you have tried in this book may have highlighted the common habit of getting set to perform an action by building up tension in the neck; this pulls the head back and down. However, this movement invariably remains hidden to the athlete and is barely noticeable to a coach observing, because he or she will see the more obvious symptoms of an unco-ordinated technique elsewhere. Efforts to change the symptoms without addressing the cause will only accomplish partial, if any, success. I have seen many cases where preventing even the tiniest unnecessary action achieves significant improvements in perform-ance. The key point here is that continuous performance enhance-ment requires a diligent, mindful attitude whilst training, so you become aware of these small actions that may prevent an optimum performance and time in The Zone.

Setting goals

Although I have written about the need to go into the unknown to get into The Zone, this doesn't prevent you from setting goals; that is, something that represents where you would like to be.

A goal is a wish to achieve something you regard as worthwhile, that represents a challenge. It will be a target beyond your current achievements requiring a substantial commitment on your behalf to attain. Once you have reached your goal it will be something to take pride in and will drive you on to achieve a higher level. Your wish is the known part.

The unknown part is the journey you will have to make to take you to where you want to be. Your goal represents somewhere you have yet to go, so you will not yet know exactly what will be required from you to achieve it.

Obviously it will involve time and effort to make the necessary improvements, but you will not know how you are going to respond to these demands and more importantly, just how far you can go. If you do only what you know, there is a danger of setting out a plan based on more of the same sort of training that may actually be limiting your progress. A good example here is the case of a runner who wants to break the four-minute mile. He could devise a training plan to increase stamina and speed, but fail to assess whether his technique is efficient. All of his training to reach this goal is based around his habitual running style that will be assumed to be right, because that is how he has always run. Perhaps a better way to approach achieving this goal would be to include a step to review his running style and experiment with technique. A good place to start would be to focus on the present, get into The Zone and see what emerges.

A conventional training plan of 'more of the same' makes the big assumption that the running is fine and with a bit of determination everything will fall into place. The goal may be reached, but his running technique has been reinforced by the additional training and the perception that it must be good because he has used it to run the four-minute mile, whether efficient or not. And at what long-term cost to his body? An opportunity has been lost for development because he has only done what he already knows, except with more effort.

Whether conscious of it or not, you will have a goal in mind that determines what you do. It may be for a quiet, comfortable life, to earn more money, look good, get fit or all of these. I believe it is important to have goals as a way to motivate and encourage continuous self-improvement, but the goal itself must be carefully thought out before you set off on your journey toward it.

A goal should …
- be something you know is achievable and provides you with the motivation to train.

- be something you can take responsibility for. You own it and only you can make it happen or fail. Others may be involved, such as in a team event, but each must know their part.

- have a specific target so you know when you have achieved it; for example, completing a 10 k run, making the first team or getting a black belt in a martial art.

- involve doing an activity you can enjoy and benefit from.

- be shared with the people around you so they will ask you about your progress, adding to your motivation.

- involve your family and friends - discuss it with them; ensure there are no conflicts, and gain their support.

- be broken down into smaller tangible steps so each stage represents a tick in a box, allowing you to take satisfaction from the journey.

- provide you with the opportunity to experiment and learn.

- challenge your intellect as well as your body.

A goal should not be ...
- impossible or unrealistic

- plucked out of the air just because it sounds good. 'I want to run a marathon' is fine if you like running and are prepared to put in the time, but if you are not going to enjoy the months of training that lie ahead it is not a good goal to set.

- given an arbitrary target without any meaning, such as increasing your trips to the gym to 4 times a week; this doesn't meet the criteria of the should be's above. However, this might be a subset of a goal that will enable you to achieve the big one.

- too easy and require little effort.

- set in concrete and be non-negotiable. Be prepared to re-assess your goal and your reasons for achieving it. Don't suffer needlessly and struggle to achieve a goal that will adversely affect you, your family and your friends.

- detrimental to your health.

Once you have decided on your goal, ask the following questions to clarify your reasons for selecting it.

Why do I want to achieve this? This could be any reason from giving you the motivation to get out of bed in the morning, right up to achieving fame and fortune.

How will I benefit from pursing this goal? Will the reward justify the time and money you will need to commit to succeed? If your goal provides the opportunity for self-improvement then the answer has to be yes.

How will I know when I have succeeded? Have you set a definite finishing point, target or time limit? Can it be measured?

When you are satisfied with your answers write down your goal and then underneath add '**How I am going to achieve this**.' This will include steps to take you closer each day to your ultimate goal. List everything that needs to be done in preparation, no matter how mundane. Your list may include steps like these:

- buying new kit
- research
- finding useful sources of information/ advice
- getting professional help
- joining a sports club
- getting a check-up from your doctor

Be sure that each step on your action plan is clear and contains just one action, so you can tick the box when it's done. Be methodical about your preparation and do not be tempted to rush straight into your training. The well-known business mantra is just as applicable here – proper planning prevents p*** poor performance! Be in the moment when writing down your plan and allow yourself time to think the thing through before committing time and effort to achieving it. A good plan also helps you keep your mind focused on the task in hand, increasing your chances of success. When you do achieve your goal you can also take satisfaction in your planning and application of that plan.

I would advise you to add two specific steps to your plan.

Firstly, include the step to assess how you are moving and your overall technique. Do not take your technique for granted and assume it is adequate to meet your target. You can do this using the procedures covered in this book, and by making your objective for each training session to focus on the present activity – so you will get into The Zone. If you do this on every outing, through experience you will get better at knowing where to place your awareness to get into the moment.

Secondly, and just as important, set time aside to reflect on your progress, method and how your goal is fitting in with your life. It is essential to keep some perspective on what you are doing and how it is affecting those around you. If you are devoting a considerable amount of time to achieving your ambition, is it still worthwhile? You may schedule in specific time or activity for reflection. Some people go fishing; many top sports people choose a different sport - golf is quite a popular choice. Whatever the activity, ensure it is some-thing where you can take time out, lose yourself a little and let the thoughts flow. Don't make it something you have to plan in detail or something that has other goals associated with it. If you are going to fish don't set a target to catch ten in one afternoon!

Observe, think, act, achieve

At this stage all you have in front of you is a sheet of paper with your goal at the top and listed beneath, your individual steps to get there plus your time out activity. Put this in a place where it can be seen. Keep a training diary and include what you have done, how you have done it, what you learnt and whether you feel you could do it differently. I also like to estimate before training what I think I could achieve; for example, if I feel great I estimate what time my three-mile run will be. Alternatively, if I don't feel in top form and have to push myself to go for a run, what could my time be then? This is a useful process as you may find that how you feel does not always translate into the quality of your performance. Some of my best sessions are often when I initially thought I wouldn't train - yet more evidence of unknown factors that can affect performance.

Another vital technique for reaching your goal is to assess constantly what you want to achieve - your approach, methods and technique. Are you progressing? Is your time spent training productive? Are you varying your program or cross training? If your goal is to run a marathon you can still work on short sprints and change the distance and speed you run. If you always run 5, 10 or 18 miles at the same speed, you will get less and less from each run.

If you compete at any level with your sport, performance enhancement is obviously about getting better at what you do, because they don't hand out medals for being the most content athlete on the track – if they did would you want it? But performance enhancement is not about pushing yourself harder in an attempt to squeeze that little bit extra out of your body. It's about training smarter and playing the role of a scientist to develop theories, ask questions, observe and assess outcomes of your actions. Try things that you wouldn't normally consider. Some of the best discoveries in science have been made by accident. I often ask runners to see how much effort they can take out of their action without slowing down. Some comment it feels like cheating because they are still moving at speed but it's not them doing it!

Your comfortable habits remain one of the biggest obstacles to performance enhancement. The habit of trying too hard can lead to unnecessary effort, imposing additional muscular activity over and above your body's attempts to coordinate itself. These actions will not get you into The Zone. Maintain a curiosity about your body; what you can do with it and how; and your enthusiasm for your sport and performance will soar. This is half the battle to continuous performance enhancement.

You do need to be challenged under different circumstances to keep you interested, and your body will learn to adapt to the varying conditions. Appreciate the difference between challenging and pushing yourself to the limits. By all means take yourself into the unknown by trying something new and going further than perhaps you normally would, but know when to stop. For instance, you may wish to run at your top speed for a little extra distance and observe what effect this has on you. Do you start pulling unnecessary faces and lifting your shoulders? Can you start moving more efficiently when you have little energy left in reserve? I find this a very useful technique so long as you stay in the moment, keep observing and make an informed decision of whether to stop or sustain your time in the unknown for a little longer.

Goal or Millstone?

Is your goal still appropriate? If you feel it is too big and not achievable in the time period you would like, adjust it. Do not see this as a set back. It is a sensible, reasoned step to take and could still help you achieve the ultimate target. Frustration at your perceived lack of progress is never going to help you reach your goal. Stay hungry but don't become discouraged and disillusioned. If you don't make the first team and end up giving up your sport due to the frustration, your initial goal has become an obstruction in your development. If you decide to change sport, do it for the right reasons and not because of negative thoughts. Your goal should not become an all-consuming obsession that excludes everything else, because if you don't achieve it where does that leave you? You would get little enjoyment from your success if you have alienated your friends and family in the process. Success is not much fun if you have no one to share it with. Pursuit of your goal should change you for the better. If you are becoming obsessed and cannot talk about anything else, it is time to reflect a little more on your reasons for achieving this goal. If you get to this stage take a break.

Follow the right way to achieving your goal and you will discover that what you gain from the journey will be beneficial in many other ways. Learn from your training and be prepared to change things. If what you are doing isn't working, don't train harder with the same methods;

train smarter, go back to your plan and rework your program.

You may choose to promise yourself a reward on successful completion but do make it relevant to your long-term goals. A weekend trip to a glamorous city to run a marathon would give your motivation for running a shot in the arm; whereas an all-you-can-eat meal on reaching your target weight would obviously set you back into bad habits. However, if you have chosen an appropriate goal and planned accordingly, the experience of the journey and achievement in itself will mean more than anything – although it's nice to have some icing on your cake!

Whatever discipline or activity you use, focus on the activity and your application rather than being distracted by the desired goal. Make it the focus of each training session to get into the moment and be aware of the process and you will reach your target. Your goal is the end of your journey but don't forget to enjoy the ride.

A young boy travelled across Japan to the school of a famous martial artist. When he arrived at the dojo (school) he was given an audience by the Sensei (teacher.) "What do you wish from me?" the master asked.

> *"I wish to be your student and become the finest karate student in the land," the boy replied. "How long must I study?"*
>
> *"Ten years at least," the master answered.*
>
> *"Ten years is a long time," said the boy. "What if I studied twice as hard as all your other students?"*
>
> *"Twenty years," replied the master.*
>
> *"Twenty years! What if I practice day and night with all my effort?"*
>
> *"Thirty years," was the master's reply.*
>
> *"How is it that each time I say I will work harder, you tell me that it will take longer?" the boy asked.*
>
> *"The answer is clear. When one eye is fixed upon your destination, there is only one eye left with which to find the way."*

Grace Under Pressure

Pressure by itself will not keep you out of The Zone, but how you react to it will make a difference. It is possible to learn how to handle the stress of the big event in a way that will take you into the optimum state for a peak performance. Our ancestors' survival mechanism for dangerous situations may be detrimental for the office worker, but it's still appropriate for the demands of competitive sport.

Whether you compete or just train for 'fun', there will be pressure on you to deliver. Pressure may come from outside such as the press, the public, your coach, your family and friends, and also from the inside, depending on your own expectations. How do you respond to this sort of situation? Stress is relative. A ten year old competing in their first organised event would find it just as demanding as an experienced athlete would find an Olympic final.

What separates the elite from the rest on the big occasions is how they handle it. It is important to recognise that stress is not the situation; it is your reaction to it. Your body will respond appropriately to how you perceive your circumstances. If you are on the start line looking down the track your muscles will need to be ready to fire. The stress hormones adrenaline and cortisol should be flooding your system in anticipation for what is to come; after all, you are not curled up in front of the fire with a mug of cocoa. You are about to put all your training to the test and pit yourself against others who want exactly what you want and just as badly. Your stress response will put you on high alert and in the perfect state to compete at your highest possible level, if you do not allow yourself the wrong kind of reaction. If you allow the pressure to go to your neck and shoulder muscles you will apply the brakes whilst your engine is revving and ready to go.

Rise to the occasion. Enjoy the thrill and the rush that comes from the pressure. Stay in the moment and put your situation into perspective. Remember why you are there; you want to be there because this is what you have trained for. You are not going into battle where you might get seriously injured or worse. This is the moment you can excel at what you do best and test yourself to your limit. You can learn a lot about yourself when it comes to the crunch.

When my son was about to take his first aikido grading he told me that he felt very nervous. I asked him to compare this new sensation with what it was like when he was bored. This was the total opposite as he was now experiencing what it was like to fire on all cylinders ready for a challenge. I don't know whether my little pep talk made a difference – how many of us listen to our parents? - but he passed with flying colours.

Many athletes report their best performances come when the pressure is on. The athlete who can learn to inhibit a detrimental response to the situation is ideally prepared for competition - a heightened state of readiness and alertness, and a body ready to release its explosive power combined with poise.

7 Running in The Zone

Regardless of your sport, you probably run – either as part of the game or in a training program. Running is an excellent activity for developing and maintaining fitness. For our purposes it also provides an ideal opportunity to practise getting in the moment, to open the gateway to The Zone. Whatever your experience of running I would like you to approach the program in this chapter as a beginner. You may already have the most efficient running technique on the planet, but the objective here is to practise techniques that will get you into The Zone and see what happens to your running when you do.

Habit is double-edged sword for those wishing to get into The Zone. Habits contain the learnt behaviour patterns for your sport which is great when you're in the right frame of mind. However it can be too easy to switch off and perform with your mind elsewhere, and not in the moment where it needs to be for getting into The Zone. Habits can lead to laziness in thinking and as a result cancel out the influence of your most important resource for development – your intellect. How you run and the amount of effort you apply is dictated by your past experience. Your running habit will be called into play every time you run. Hence nothing will change if you do not experiment with your approach. If you only experience The Zone occasionally whilst running, you are probably trapped in your running matrix and are not focusing on the true activity in hand.

If you are training currently for a race and have a deadline, I suggest you wait until after the event and start this program during your natural rest period. This program is designed for you to learn the necessary skills to get you into The Zone and not specifically to get you running, although there obviously will be benefits for your style.

We will start by looking at the basic building blocks of running, so we can break down the action and provide you with the appropriate focus. Remember, to get into The Zone you have to be in the moment so you can become immersed and focused on the activity. I would like to stress the activity is not running or to be exact what your concept of running may be. The activity is the movement of your limbs to push the ground away in order to propel yourself forward at speed. Much of the activity during a stride cycle requires little or no effort, relying instead on your momentum from earlier activity, the location of joints, and your interaction with the ground. Many runners can benefit from learning to let go at the right time to reduce interference, save energy and develop an efficient style.

The following activities may help you to assess your technique but more importantly, give you a focus when you run.

Activity: *Pendulums*

I mentioned earlier that much of the activity of running requires less effort than you think. One of these is the leg swing, a movement that makes up a considerable amount of the action.

1 Sit on the edge of a table so the whole of your upper legs down to the knees are in contact.

2 Bring back your left leg until it is underneath the table and then let it go so it swings forward. It is important to let it go and not to swing it forward yourself.

3 Let alternate legs swing with minimal effort (just give them a little nudge) and think of each leg as a pendulum. If you are experiencing the need to make them swing by using your hamstrings or quadriceps, think of the space at the back of your knee joint and let go from there.

Let's try a similar experiment with your arms.

1   Stand and think of a line from the tip of your shoulders through the biceps, down the arm to your thumbs. Or just think 'long arms'.

2   As with the legs, see if you can get your arms swinging straight and by your side with a minimal effort without lifting your shoulders.

3   Now let your arms bend at the elbow; place your thumb lightly on your index finger, keep your fingers relaxed and again swing your arms without the shoulders lifting. Your hands should be relaxed, nether clenched into a fist or fingers held straight. These actions of your limbs will help to propel you forward whilst running but require less effort than most runners use.

Activity: *Backs to the Wall*

1   Stand with your back to a wall with your only your shoulder blades and buttocks making contact. You will need to stand with your heels away from the wall. The distance depends on the tone in your gluteus maximus! The back of your head does not touch the wall and should be resting on top of your spine – remember the nodding donkey.

2   Allow yourself to stand tall (just think this, don't do it) and appreciate the floor pushing back up. Be aware of the location of the hip, knee and ankle joint of your left leg.

3   Imagine a thread attached to your left knee and allow your leg to release from the hip and ankle joint and allow the thread to pull the knee forward.

4   Roll onto the ball of the left foot without taking the weight off it. Your pelvis should neither drop or lose contact with the wall – but don't push back. If you have pulled forward or dropped the pelvis you are not releasing from the hip joint.

5   Hold this position for a few moments and be aware of the contact with the floor and wall. Focus on the support you are getting from the right foot and think from the sole up through your right leg, up your back, right to the top of your head.

6 Slowly let your knee come back so your left heel returns to the floor, and be aware of the responding push that comes as your shin bones straighten and push back up through your thigh bone.

Repeat on the opposite side and when you are able to do this without swaying or losing contact with the wall, start to increase the speed until closer to walking speed. This activity is very useful for running as it allows you to appreciate how to allow your legs to swing without undue movement of the pelvis.

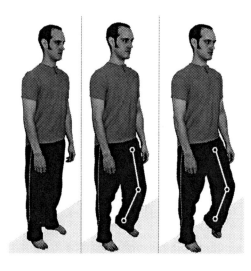

Fig 7.1 Use the wall only as reference to whether you are moving the pelvis to move your leg. You should not push back or lean against the wall.

Activity: *Walk the Walk*

You are now going to put together the previous activities and take them into walking; after all you don't want to run before you can walk.

1 Use the same technique from the activity in Chapter 4; one small step, to initiate walking forward.

2 Be aware of the movement in your hip, knee and ankle joints, as learnt from activity you have just completed, to allow your legs to swing from the hip and your lower leg to release from the knee. The pendulums activity will have shown you how little work is required to swing the lower legs and arms.

3   See how much effort you can take out of the act of walking and just allow your limbs to swing.

4   Think about releasing muscles and joints rather than the effort involved.

5   Be aware of the ground beneath your feet and think of 'walking tall' by using the upward thrust from the ground in response to your body weight coming down.

6   Start slowly and start to build up speed – but not by trying harder. To increase your speed let your arms swing a little faster but without lifting your shoulders. If you can leave your legs alone they will increase speed to match your arms so you will be moving faster without the effort you probably think is necessary.

Fig 7.2 Compare the poised, upright runners on the right with the two on the left who are using their neck and shoulder muscles inappropriately. Do you waste effort when running? How would you know?

Activity: *Walk to Run*

1   Start with an efficient walking stride as in the previous activity and build up your speed by freeing up your shoulders, to allow the arms to swing faster.

2   Think about going into a run and observe what you feel you need to do. Are you tempted to lift your shoulders? Does your neck stiffen and your head go back? Or do you feel the need to tighten your lower back to get the legs moving? You probably will have your own

interpretation of what running involves; but remember, a number of these actions may be inappropriate, reducing the efficiency of your technique, which will be carried throughout your run.

3 Avoid doing what you feel you need to do to start running, so you make the changeover from walking to running without additional effort.

4 Allow your arms to bend at the elbow and keep them swinging in a linear motion. Think of the legs swinging from the hips and raise the legs by thinking of your knees leading the move.

5 Once the knee has been raised, the lower leg can be allowed to swing through as in the pendulums activity. The kicking action of many runners increases the workload on the quadriceps, and as we shall see later, is totally unnecessary.

6 Be conscious of the hip, knee and ankle joints working together in the movement.

7 As with walking tall, think of running tall to use the force of gravity. From a practical point of view this is the ground pushing back up in response to your feet landing on it. This may sound a little strange initially, but the ground is where the force that moves you forward comes from.

8 Be cautious of trying to hold yourself up to achieve an upright position. If you can remove unnecessary effort, your body will attain an effortless upright stance due to the absence of excessive muscular activity.

Your challenge is to prevent yourself from trying to run as this will involve habitual actions you associate with running. Run for a short distance and then stop and walk for a few minutes to regain the sense of effortless movement. Alternate between walking and running whilst preventing any build up of tension in your neck, shoulders and back.

Running Philosophy

During a training session do you continue to run when uncomfortable or tired, or do you stop and walk to recover? Many runners, myself once included, consider stopping or slowing down to be a failure and admitting defeat. Unfortunately, this attitude places the emphasis on quantity rather than quality. Running when you're tired, injured or feeling unwell reduces the quality of your movement as breathing, circulation and muscle function are impaired. You will never get into The Zone in this state.

On the other hand, you must also be wary of setting up the habit of stopping just because you feel tired. There is a difference between 'pushing yourself to the limit' and taking yourself into the unknown. Pushing harder invariably means putting more of the same (extra unnecessary effort) into the run, resulting in poor form. Going into the unknown is about learning from a new experience. If you feel tired, keep running and observe whether there is too much tension in your body. If necessary stop, try to regain your focus, then start again. Do not be concerned about the time. It is more productive to use a training run to identify problems with your technique and address them, than it is just to get a good time and suffer as a result.

Realistically you cannot stop in a competitive event, but you can approach your training sessions differently. There is nothing to gain from applying a wholly competitive attitude to training. In this state, your ability to observe and learn from experience is limited and you will rarely get into The Zone this way. Muscles reflect our state of mind – if you maintain a competitive approach, the same habitual muscle tension will be present during every run. To improve performance without changing your underlying habitual patterns of how you run will require more effort; it's more of the same with extra tension. More of the wrong kind of effort increases muscular activity that will resist movement – preventing you from slipping into a flowing rhythm, into the moment and into The Zone. This brings about a more competitive attitude out of frustration if your performance is not improving. Back to square one.

In the absence of a competitive attitude, you can try things that are not feasible during a race. To stop and walk gives you time to observe what otherwise may go unnoticed if you continued to run. If you are a non-competitive runner, time is not as important as the quality of your run. Maybe you use running to supplement your training for another sport. Competing against the clock in this case could be detrimental if good form is lost chasing a meaningless personal best. You could literally be running yourself into the ground if you continue to apply more effort whilst using the same inefficient style.

Focusing purely on speed and the time will reduce what you get from your run, as discussed in Chapter 5. Something is lost from the act if the goal becomes more important than how you achieve it. Yes, running against the clock may be a useful guide for measuring improvement, but it should not solely dictate training strategy. The good times will come if you run mindfully and learn through what you observe. A more efficient technique will evolve through elimination of unnecessary effort. If you run with a stopwatch it is easy to become a slave to it. If the time is good at the half way stage, does it change your run? Equally, if the time is slow, do you speed up to make up the time? Either way the time has become the most important aspect of the run instead of maintaining attention as to how you run.

Top athletes whether sprinters, middle or long distance runners will vary their training runs alternating amongst endurance, strength and speed tests. If you don't vary your runs it not only habituates your body for one particular type of running; it can also become boring. Keep your attitude fresh by switching and mixing your program. However, regardless of what type of run you are doing, your main objective is to focus on the present so you will get into The Zone.

What do you think about when running?

A survey into what runners think about when competing identified four categories. These are relevant to participating in many sporting activities:

1 **Inward monitoring** – focusing on how you feel while running.

2 **Outward monitoring** – focusing on aspects of the race such as distance, terrain and tactics.

3 **Inward distraction** – having thoughts irrelevant to the race such as solving 'mental puzzles' or wondering what we are going to do after the race.

4 **Outward distraction** – focusing on surroundings irrelevant to the race, such as scenery.

The research concluded that inward distraction (3) should be avoided as it reduces awareness, resulting in either running too fast and 'burning out' or running too slowly. Inward monitoring (1) is useful for judging the required pace and also for being aware of any warning signals such as muscle strain. The researchers believe that the most attention should be focused outwardly on aspects of the race, to minimise the influence of discomfort whilst remaining aware of the race situation.

I would like to add a fifth category; I call it interactive awareness. This is thinking of how you are running. This is not to be confused with what you are feeling or doing in the race, but to the actual movement in relation to yourself and your surroundings. For example, when running are you aware of the location of your hip and shoulder joints or the active role the ground is playing in your movement? Focusing on the act, as you know, will bring you into the present and can help to 'free up' the movement – if you can recognise what you're doing and then stop putting in unnecessary effort.

This type of thinking is neither inward nor outward; it's both, as it requires you to maintain awareness of who is running, how you are running and where you are running. For example, if you are aware of the feet landing on the ground when running, you can appreciate the force opposing your weight as the push back helps you to move forward. The upward push is translated into a forward motion by the action of hip, knee and ankle joints in conjunction with the movement of your arms.

Newton's third law of gravity states that 'the mutual actions of two bodies upon each other are always equal and in opposite directions', or more commonly known as, 'for every action there is an equal opposite reaction'. You do not have to be pulled down by gravity; yet many runners appear to lose the battle. Contemplate this law when running and you can allow yourself to 'go up' – to go forward due to the action of the legs and use this force to your advantage.

> *"Focusing on the moment means racing and thinking about what I'm doing at that moment, focusing on the things I can impact, letting go the small bobbles that always occur in any race because attention to what went wrong is energy wasted. My thoughts when running: Elbows back, lift the heels, forward, how's my breathing, aid station, water please, forward, forward, where's the competition, around the pothole, drive the knees, elbows straight back, thumbs to armpits, lift the heels, forward, forward, how's my effort, near the end there's more, hang on, hang on, only 5 more minutes and we're done, forward, lift the heels, forward, thumbs to armpits, good, good, keep it going…"*
>
> Alicia Parr, tri-athlete, on what is going through her mind as she participates in one of the most demanding sports.

Running Into The Unknown

Your approach to any type of training is susceptible to habit. If you keep doing the same things you will get the same results, yet this is exactly what most of us do. You may have a set warm-up routine or procedures to get you ready for a training session that may be absolutely right for you. Yet the question you need to ask is, if you do everything according to what feels right you will continue to perform within your matrix. So how will you know if there is a better way?

There is a theory that the evolutionary process throws up a few mutant genes occasionally, to test the water and see if the new species is better suited to the environment. You don't have to grow a third leg to improve your running (although it would be an interesting challenge!) However, it would be a beneficial just to try something completely different in your routine every now and then. But remember habit will stand in your way by making everything new seem wrong. Learn to deal with this feeling, because it means you are going in the right direction – that is, into the unknown as you move outside your matrix to experience something beyond the familiar sensations.

Try the following in place of your usual routine. If you feel you do not want to interrupt your schedule for fear of your performance suffering, you may well be a slave to habit. Leave your stopwatch at home for now to avoid giving any consideration to the time, as to do so will keep you out of the moment.

The urge to return to your normal way of running will be very strong, as this would be the most familiar. Resist the need to get it right and continue the experiment for as long as possible. Remember what you have learnt about your body from the previous experiments in this book. Let your legs release from the hip joints; your lower legs swing from the knee; your arms move without raising your shoulders; and just as important, allow the ground to push you up and forward. This may seem like a lot to think about initially but with practice it will become easier and will get you focused on the present and into The Zone. Once you are there it takes no effort at all and you will be doing all of this, and then some.

Alternate between running and walking – perhaps two minutes of each – and see if you can maintain the freedom of movement in both activities. Check that you do not get set to start running after your period of walking.

At some point during your run, allow the arms to stop swinging and drop in front of your hips – an action common with many runners. Observe what this does to your back. You will notice the back starts to twist and the shoulders to roll as the push coming up from the road needs to go somewhere. The movement of the hip flexors to lift your thighbones requires an equal action in the upper body to maintain balance and form. This unnecessary twist reduces efficiency by throwing weight in the wrong direction. Return to swinging the arms as in pendulums and observe how the twisting action disappears. You can reduce the amount of work done by the hip flexors by letting your foot bounce off the floor. When you're running the force going into the ground increases in comparison to walking, so you will get a greater push (assistance) coming back up.

Running Faster

When you want to run faster what do you need to do? Based on my experience of working with runners, I would say with confidence that much of the additional effort you put into running faster is actually working against you. Many runners effectively apply the brakes when they put in more effort and stiffen up, pull the head back and lift the shoulders. They need more effort just to maintain their current speed. You may have the sensation you are running faster because of the increased effort, but are you using that additional energy efficiently? The experiments in this book will have demonstrated how your sense of effort can be misleading and how habit dictates what you think is appropriate.

The dramatic finish of the 2000 Sydney Olympic men's triathlon is a good example. Vuckovic of Germany had quite a comfortable lead going into the last mile over second placed Canadian Simon Whitfield. Whitfield later said he was racing for the pride of Canada and was determine to catch the leader. As he started to close the gap, Vuckovic began to glance repeatedly over his shoulder. Had Vuckovic maintained his original pace over the last five hundred metres he probably would have won. Unfortunately for Germany, he became anxious of being caught and tried to increase speed. If you watch the footage of the last moments of the race you will see how his efforts to run faster actually appear to slow him down. His head went back and he tightened what must have been an exhausted body for the last push. His misdirected effort worked against him and Whitfield passed Vuckovic in the last one hundred metres to take gold.

To run faster you need to make your legs swing faster; it's obvious isn't it? Well, perhaps there is more to it. In a Harvard University study entitled 'Faster top running speeds are achieved with greater ground forces not more rapid leg movements' Weyand et al (2000) found that runners reach faster speeds not by repositioning their legs more rapidly in the air, but by other means. Head of research, Peter Weyand, explains:

> *"When you see someone running at top speed, his or her legs and arms are swinging all over the place. There is just not*

enough active muscle power available to account for all the motion you see taking place."

So where does the force come from? To determine what limits top running speed, 33 runners of varied ability were monitored performing at different speeds. Surprisingly, the amount of time taken to reposition the leg between steps (swing time) was approximately the same at top speed for all runners. The slowest runner's swing time almost matched that of the 1996 Olympic 100 metre champion, Donovan Bailey!

So if the swing time is not a factor, how do the faster runners achieve higher speeds? The researchers discovered speed is determined by the amount of force applied to the ground, rather than how fast the runner could move their legs. The greater the force, called the support force (SF,) coming down through the body to the ground results in a greater force pushing back up, called the ground reaction force (GRF.) Remember Newton's third law of gravity! So those runners putting more into the ground got more out of it. Peter Weyand again:

"Much of the work of running is done through passive mechanical processes, in which tendons and muscles act through elastic rebound, much like springs uncoiling, the uncoiling delivers the power to swing your legs."

At first this seems wrong because, surely, to run faster we need to move the legs quicker. The study suggests that extra effort applied to moving the legs faster may not therefore be the most efficient way to increase speed. The upward thrust of the GRF is translated into forward motion by the action of the hip, knee and ankle joints. I believe the act of trying to move the legs faster leads to unnecessary muscle activity; joint movement will be impeded therefore reducing the leg's efficiency to perform its task. When we run faster obviously the legs move more quickly, but this should be a result of a greater force pushing the leg back up from the earth (a recoil action.) For example, the harder you throw a tennis ball at the ground the higher and faster it bounces back up. The faster a leg comes up from the earth, the quicker it comes back down. The study summarises the results by stating:

"We conclude that human runners reach faster top speeds not by repositioning their limbs more rapidly in the air, but by applying greater support forces to the ground."

The study confirmed common knowledge that the fastest runners achieve longer strides. It has been known for many years that longer strides meant faster running and coaches have encouraged runners to practice taking longer strides. This now appears to be wrong. Trying to increase the stride length decreases a muscle's ability to apply the support force required to get back up for the next step. Runners are not faster because they take longer strides. It is the other way around; runners take longer strides because they are fast. They are fast because they apply greater support forces to the ground allowing them to spend longer time in the air, hence the longer stride.

So if the secret to achieving greater speed is to apply more force to the ground, how do we go about doing it? I believe one factor is balance. If your body is not poised and is using excessive muscular activity you may not be applying the right sort of force into the ground. You can exaggerate this to test the theory by leaning backwards as you run and seeing how you slow down. In a poised, balanced body I believe you apply forces more effectively to the ground. Combine this with the absence of tension, and the legs will free up and use the push coming back up from the floor more efficiently.

Activity: *Stepping Up The Pace*

When you want to increase your speed, try the following method:

1 First check what you normally want to do to run faster. After a minute, slow down to a comfortable jogging pace and again think about raising the pace.

2 This time do not think about running faster but instead think release and let your arms swing faster without raising your

shoulders. If you allow your arms move faster, requiring less energy, you will find your legs will match the speed.

I believe this method uses our innate segmental rolling reflexes that coordinate the upper and lower limbs for movement. If either upper or lower limbs move faster the others will have to keep up. If you can resist the urge to put in more effort to run faster, it will allow your reflexes to work and get your legs moving – invariably with less muscular activity than you would guess it would need. Try this exercise and experience the difference. The first time you speed up you will use your usual habitual method; the second time will feel different because it will be unfamiliar. When you get it working well it can feel sensational as you use the ground to go up and forward; arms and legs release; your spine lengthens; the brake comes off and you're flying. You are now in The Zone and nothing else matters.

Running Consciously

You probably will have experienced running in The Zone without knowingly doing anything mentioned here, but was it intended? You may have your own methods that take you into The Zone but I would guess that whichever way you use, it would bring you into the moment first. This is fine. However if you want to experience running in The Zone more often it cannot remain accidental.

I know many who listen to music whilst running and this works well for them. It's about getting a balance between you and your surroundings. Music doesn't work for me as I get too immersed in the music and not the true activity of running. Plus I would probably end up singing which would not only keep me out of the moment, but also anyone else within hearing distance! What's important are balance and focus. I believe the added advantage of focusing on your movement not only takes you into The Zone but also helps with the continuous process of improvement. If you can't measure you can't manage, so the more you can become aware of your actions the better placed you are to make amendments where necessary. It also makes training far more challenging (and therefore more interesting and enjoyable) if you remain aware of yourself, stay in the present and do not switch off your thinking part just because it's 'physical' activity.

This subtle change in attitude opens up a whole new aspect to your training as it becomes more than just trying to improve your times or distances. You can now assess continuously the impact of what you are thinking in relation to your technique and performance in real-time, making small adjustments and being able instantly to judge their effectiveness. Remember that one of the seven Zone characteristics discussed in Chapter 2 is feeling a deep passion for the activity driving you on to higher levels of performance, which in turn makes this experience provide further inspiration; it becomes self-perpetuating. If you take the mindful approach to your training, knowing your informed decisions have led to real improvements enhances the reward for your activity.

The benefits will not be limited to performance but also to your appreciation of the activity, application and approach. If you can do something well, and what's more, know why you can do it well, your whole self is integrated, working at an optimum level to achieve a worthwhile goal. You can take the full credit for a great performance because you consciously have made the decisions and executed your plans accordingly. If you throw a dart at a dartboard randomly there is no point celebrating when you hit the bull's eye! Take full control of your actions and running becomes more than just a way to keep fit or a competitive event. It has now become an activity for learning, experimenting and, perhaps even more importantly, really to enjoy.

Whilst I cannot claim to get into The Zone every time I run, I do spend more time in it than out of it by using the techniques described in this book. It's a continual process of observation and experimentation and recognizing that I can still get it all wrong. On the occasions when it does go badly I can still use these methods to understand why.

8 When It Goes Wrong and How To Move On

It would be naive to believe that during a lifetime of sporting activity you will not experience disappointment or frustration at some stage. After all, there would be no highs without the lows. Most of us will go through a phase of poor form, loss of confidence in ability, lack of motivation or the dreaded curse of a sports injury. These periods only become a problem when they are prolonged, when an injury is persistent or when it becomes a constant condition. Yet no player becomes a bad player overnight.

If you had the skills and attitude that have got you so far, they will still be there. The question is, why they have temporarily stopped working for you. Either you are doing something that is interfering with your natural ability; or it could be the case of going as far as you can with your current methods – that is, your habits. If you are experiencing a drop in your performance you have to stop before doing anything else. If banging your head against a brick wall isn't working, don't bang it harder!

Whilst these lows represent the opposite of The Zone, they provide the perfect time to assess your motives, attitude and technique so you can move on. This is an important point – to move on. How often do you hear sports people say they just want to get back to where they were before the loss of form/injury/incident? But do they really want to go back and set in motion the same process that led to their current predicament?

To attempt a return to form or regain confidence by turning back the clock will not get to the cause. What's done is done and what you have accomplished will have been in the confidence that you were right. How many times do you do things that you know are wrong? The decisions you make, whether conscious or not, are based on what you believe to be right. From when you train and what you do, to the decisions you make in play, you refer to your previous experiences. But remember this is what got you to where you are today and if you are injured, lacking in confidence and form or stuck at a plateau, it's not a route you want to go down again. This is the perfect time to put behind you what has happened and reassess your approach, technique and application so you can make the changes that will get you out of your current state.

Injury

Let's start by looking at injury. It is frustrating if you cannot train due to an injury. But it is more frustrating to return too early, under-perform and complicate the injury further, because it will take longer to recover. Be patient and use the time to learn about your injury, ask your therapist or read up on your condition.

If it's a non-contact injury:

- What are the possible causes?

- Could it have been avoided?

- Was it self-inflicted by over-training, poor technique or a bad decision?

- What can you do to help with the recovery process?

Take responsibility for yourself and don't leave it all for your therapist. He or she is not repairing your car that you leave at the garage and pick up after it's done. Learn more about your body so once you are fit enough to return to your training, you will have a good understanding of how to use yourself better. Your body doesn't come with an instruction manual (which we probably wouldn't read anyway) so take time to experiment with movement, such as the procedures in this book.

We are told 'if it ain't bust don't fix it', but in the case of our bodies they may be 'bust' long before we realise it. Percy Cerutty, the trial-blazing Australian running coach, had better advice. He encouraged his athletes to be aware of their bodies. He would say 'if you can hear the whispers you never have to hear the screams'.

You may have heard the term feedback training. It is a method being used increasingly for training that encourages the athlete to feel, and associate that feeling with the movement and outcome. However, what you perceive is happening is not a constant. What you feel one day will differ from another depending on numerous factors, many of which you may be unaware of.

I return to the habitual patterns involving the neck muscles, for example. If you are oblivious to these habitual patterns, how will you know if the tension is greater in your neck one day and absent the next? The amount of muscular activity in this area will affect what you feel elsewhere in your body. You may notice a difference in your movement; that is, it will feel easier due to improved coordi-nation because you neck reflexes are working without interference, but you won't always know why. If the cause is not known it cannot be managed. A truly great performance is then down to luck of the draw of whether you are unknowingly stiffening your neck or not. The importance of knowing how to stop and reduce all the habitual 'background noise' of your nervous system becomes more obvious.

Exercise Your Right To Remain Silent

Even a few weeks' break from training will begin to tell on your return. It is essential not to try and make up for lost time following an injury. You have to accept you are not going to pick up where you left off. Take the injury as a warning things were not going as well as they could have been, and change your approach. In the first chapter we looked at change and how this means 'going into the unknown' because your habits will feel right and comfortable. Real change can only happen if you can first learn how to stop – see later in this chapter. If you regularly do exercises ask yourself whether they are really helping to improve your movement. Stop for a period and see if it makes any difference. You only have a limited time to train so it is worth checking you are not wasting a percentage on needless exercises.

If you are suffering from recurring injuries something has to change, and in most cases I would suggest it's the exercise program that has to go. It is common for us to assume the exercise approach is right and therefore to increase our program in the belief that more must be better. I have seen dramatic improvement where people have stopped doing their exercises altogether and instead trained smarter in their sport, or added another activity such as swimming or running. I used to do over five hundred sit-ups a day in various positions, but I never stopped to think how it actually helped my performance in sport.

What are your exercises doing for you? Are they reinforcing your bad habits by using your neck and back muscles poorly? Is the emphasis on individual muscles? Did your therapist identify a weakness in muscles essential for your sport? If yes, how long had you been playing your sport? Either you are not performing the movements of your sport correctly, or your therapist is wrong. If you have been playing your sport for sometime then shouldn't you have the strength in these muscles? If you do have a weakness then you are doing something wrong in your sport and the prescribed exercises will not ultimately change how you move. This is down to your concepts and coordination – neither will be addressed by corrective exercises that have nothing in common the movements of your sport.

Even if you feel you were in no way to blame for your injury, such as a contact injury, you can still use this period to assess your technique and approach. If your injury was a result of a collision, you were definitely not in The Zone at the time. You could use your enforced rest period to experiment with the procedures below to get you there more often and prevent this sort of injury.

Loss of Confidence and Form

The reason for a sudden drop in form or loss of confidence can be harder to identify if an obviously disastrous performance has not shattered your self-belief. Confidence is a tricky element to define. People may be confident but have no apparent reason to feel it other than an exaggerated opinion of their ability. You probably know someone who fits into this category. With no justification they will be the most confident person on the pitch (and they usually have the best kit.) What they perceive of their performance is very different from reality and everyone else's assessment. However, should they be told about the discrepancy? Or is it better to leave them in blissful ignorance and wait for the bubble to burst? Of course this category could also include you or I, because we also can deceive ourselves! How would we know? As far as we are concerned we trust what we believe because we have no other way of getting information from the outside world that bypasses our senses and perceptions. Within our matrix there are no wrong perceptions – think about it.

In contrast, many gifted athletes can experience a crisis of confidence even when the reality of their results tells a different story. They will require constant encouragement and positive feedback and for some this is sufficient to reinforce their worth, yet others will still not accept or believe it. Lastly, there are a few who can justify their confidence in their ability and in rare cases can maintain a balance between their form and perception of themselves throughout their lives. Whatever you think will influence how you approach your per-formance, and will therefore become a factor. If it is lacking, you will never get into The Zone.

Get A Grip On Reality

The confidence issue highlights a feature of performance that gets little attention. This is a discrepancy between what we perceive happens and what actually happens – we could call it a 'reality gap.' For example, you will have the intention to carry out an act such as getting out of the chair. You will subconsciously arrange yourself to get the weight onto your feet to activate the muscles in the legs but be unaware of what is actually happening. You may also have discovered from the previous experiments in this book that you were doing other actions such as stiffening your neck, shoulders and/or back. You perceive you are getting out of a chair to answer the telephone but far more is actually happening. The additional actions you unknowingly perform are not needed. In fact they make movement harder; but many people perform them and are unaware of their presence.

So you may only be aware of half of what you actually do to perform an action. If you are doing the things you have always done to get results, but find that now they no longer work, your confidence will take a knock. Yet your lack of form may be due to poor actions that have gradually crept into your technique. You will not be aware of these and therefore will no longer be doing what you thought you were doing – hence the different outcome. The harder you try, the more you could be adding unnecessary actions and the more your performance will continue to dip. We wouldn't expect a pilot to be able to fly a plane by referring to only half the instruments, yet we assume we can make the appropriate changes to our technique with a large part of the data absent from our perceptions.

Let's look at an example of a golfer, although this process can happen in any sport. A golfer starts to pull the ball off the tee (right-handed golfer hits the ball off to his left,) whereas previously the ball went straight down the fairway. Up until now his swing was free from tension, because he had stayed poised to play the stroke. Once he started to compete at a higher level, stress became a factor resulting in a small, unperceivable amount of tension in his neck and shoulders. He doesn't notice this now because he is concentrating on getting the ball toward the green. Gradually this tension becomes part of his technique because he has conditioned himself to do it, and he will not start his swing until this tension is present because he now associates this feeling with preparation.

So he will unconsciously prepare for his stroke by tightening the neck and shoulders in anticipation of the effort required. The first notice-able indication he has of the problem is the ball landing in the rough and not the feeling of tension, because this is now an automatic habit so it will be ignored. However he now knows something is wrong and will try to alter his swing. But his attempts to correct the problem start too far down the chain by focusing on the execution of the act and not his preparation or concept of it. His focus on the swing adds more tension to his habit for preparation and will start to pull the ball further.

Other alterations made will complicate the issue further, because they are now 'built' on top of his suspect preparation habits, taking him further away from his natural style. He will do what feels right; but remember the arm-folding experiment at the start of the book? The more he tries to be right the more he will rely on his comfortable habit of getting set for the shot. Confidence will obviously take a dive because he can no longer trust his judgement or his ability to make adjustments. If he is oblivious to these actions in his technique he will not be able to change them.

Things will get worse when he seeks the help of a coach. The coach will see the build up of unnecessary tension and instruct him not to do it. Our golfer's confidence will be further dented when he is told not to do something that feels right to him. When he tries to carry out what he has been told to do it will feel wrong, just as the opposite arm-fold does, and he will start to believe he doesn't know anything about golf.

The initial problem started because he was not in The Zone. Once he started to focus on an action that was yet to happen – the club making contact with the ball, he was no longer in the moment. He should have been absorbed in the act of his stance so he would be poised before he started to raise the club and rotate his body. This way he instantly would have recognised the tension and could have let it go before starting the swing.

Sports people devise all sorts of methods to stay in the moment; for example, marksmen often observe their breathing to help them focus. Yet as soon as you start to concentrate disproportionately on the desired outcome ahead of where you currently are – e.g. the seconds on the clock, the finish line or the ball going down the hole – you are taken out of the moment and inappropriate actions may begin to creep in until they become part of the technique. This does not mean the finish line is not important (of course it is) but you should not let the end of the race distract you from your current action.

Making It So

How do we define skill? Michael Wade, professor of Kinesiology and Human Factors defines skill as that which minimises the discrepancy between intent and outcome. You can said be skilled in something if you can carry out your intentions with little or no margin of error. To achieve a reduction in the discrepancy you first must have an accurate picture of what needs to be done, and then be able to monitor what is actually happening as you work to bring about the outcome. Again you will see the importance of being in the moment.

If you are focused on the result, something that has yet to happen, you will lose a sense of what is happening in between, and you are no longer in the moment. If we return to the chair experiment, your perception of time alters if you are aware of the intermediate stages of the movement, compared with when you focus purely on the reason for getting up – for example, where did I leave the phone? Even if both events take the same amount of time, subjects report a difference when estimating the duration of the event.

One good example of this is when footballer John Barnes scored one of the most breathtaking individual goals ever seen against Brazil in 1984. His speed and agility on the ball allowed him to beat half of the Brazilian team and casually tap the ball into the net. He was not aware of the enormity of his feat until after the game when he watched the game on television. His own experience of the movement was just taking a ball around one player, moving on, deciding where to go next, beating the next player and so on until he found himself with only the goal-keeper to beat. He was in the moment, and undoubtely in The Zone, which made time for him to think out his next move carefully and outwit his opponents.

Confidence comes from consistency of performance. Confidence also comes from knowing that you have made the right decisions leading to the actions that bring reliability and performance improvement. Once you develop 'conscious' consistency, that is, knowing how you achieve a good performance, your confidence in your ability grows allowing you to continue the process of improvement. By eradicating the 'unconscious' inconsistencies, such as stiffening your neck and unnecessary muscular preparations, you are better placed to observe what are you doing and make the appropriate decisions. One of my pupils refers to this as increasing the range of his radar, because the more he practises being in the moment, the more he becomes aware of the seemingly small actions that can make a big difference once he can stop doing them.

Learning To Stop

'If you want something done, ask a busy person'. Sports people are busy people and generally have great difficulty just stopping. The demands of your sport or the strict training schedule you have set yourself make it seem impossible to take time off. How many people do you know who struggle on with a persistent injury? They may never regain the sort of form they achieved before but still insist they cannot afford to stop. Yet taking time out can pay big dividends if you can discover why you have been getting injured or why your performance has dipped. An artist can stop, take a step back and see her work from a different viewpoint before deciding what to do next. If you have your nose right up against the canvas you will never see the whole picture. Taking a step back can help you to move on. A rest period is an opportunity to assess not just your technique but also your approach, motives and goals. Learn to train smarter, not harder!

Stopping doesn't mean putting your feet up and waiting for your problem to disappear by itself. There is a process that has to be followed. First you have to accept that something has gone wrong and treat it as a learning experience. Recriminations at this point are damaging and pointless – what's done is done. You can't go back and change that. If what you were doing got you into this situation you should conclude it was not the best approach. Too many people just try harder using the same methods and attitude with extra effort thrown in. It won't work. If you keep driving along the same route and arrive at the wrong destination, it doesn't make sense to go back and then follow the same route again – this time faster. You may find out more quickly that you've got it wrong, but don't waste time doing it again. Stop and consult the map!

Change cannot happen without first coming to a halt. Trying to change without at first stopping is like trying to do maintenance on an airliner whilst it's still in flight. If you are trying to make changes during your usual training regime, you will be surrounded by the same stimuli triggering your habitual reactions that are leading to your current problem. Take a step away from this environment for a period and learn to quieten things down before returning to training. When you do return, your poor habits will now hit you like a speeding train – whereas previously they were an integral part of your technique.

Stopping does not mean relaxing. Relaxation techniques are popular with many sports people but it is possible to go too far and switch off completely. Studies have found that individuals respond differently to the challenge of competition. Some perform better when stressed or 'fired-up' and do less well when they have used relaxation techniques.

The first activity here is a great place to start learning how to stop. It does involve lying down but please think of this as an activity and not a chance to sleep.

Activity: *The Full Back*

This is an extremely useful activity requiring only a little space and time and provides an excellent opportunity to stop. Twenty to twenty-five minutes each day is recommended. The purpose of the books (see diagram) is to keep the spine in its natural alignment so the neck is not pulled back by the head resting on the floor. To determine the height of the books stand with your shoulder blades touching a wall with the head sitting on top of the spine. Get someone to measure the gap between the base of the skull and the wall – this is the depth of books you will require.

1 Lie on your back on a surface that's comfortable but not too soft, head supported by a small pile of books, with the knees up.

2 For the first few minutes, just spend time being aware of the floor and where you are making contact with it – the back of your head, shoulder blades, elbows, pelvis and feet (specifically think of letting the heels drop whilst keeping the toes in contact with the floor.) Allow yourself to be supported by the floor but do not try to push yourself into it.

3 Notice the space between your torso and your arms and allow your ribs to move into these areas as you breath. This means letting the ribs move sideways; but do not attempt to make it happen as this will lead to inappropriate muscular effort. Because you are lying down you will not need large amounts of oxygen. Let the incoming air inflate the lungs and move your ribs. Let the movement of your ribs move your hands.

4 Be aware of yourself lying on the floor and just letting the air flow in and out of your nose. In the horizontal position, the weight of your skull is no longer resting on the spine so the intervertebral disks will start to thicken and the spine will lengthen.

5 Think of releasing any tension in the muscles of the torso and allow the spine to lengthen. This will 'push' your head away from your pelvis and your knees up towards the ceiling.

6 Check that you are not holding any tension in your body unnecessarily, and allow the floor to support you. By releasing the habitual patterns in this position, gravity will re-align your body and remove the strains and twists the day has put there. Most people have a tendency to contract and tighten the body. In this position think of releasing out from your centre, so your arms and legs can 'grow'.

7 When you are able to maintain awareness of your body and your breathing, slowly lift one arm and move gently whilst remaining attentive to your shoulder blades resting on the floor. Try a slow rotation with your arm bent at the elbow and think of the ball moving in the shoulder socket. Do not allow the shoulder blade to come off the floor. Repeat with the other arm.

8 Now let one leg slide across the floor and rest the weight of the leg on the heel, calf and back of the thigh. Be aware of the hip, knee and ankle joints and the three parts of the leg. Let the leg rest in this position for a few moments.

9 Return the leg to the starting position but do not to tighten your stomach. Think of the knee going up and the heel coming back toward the base of your pelvis.

Do try to spend twenty minutes a day in this position as it has many benefits. If you find your mind has wandered off to other thoughts, bring your focus back to the points where you are making contact with the floor, and to your breathing, in other words – be in the moment. The focus and stillness you can develop in this position can be taken into more and more physical activities with practice.

Fig 8.1 Taking the day out of your body.

Stopping allows you to get to know yourself a little better. You need to discover what thoughts bring about freer actions, and those that result in the opposite. Experience the stillness that can be achieved in these activities, and learn to take it into more demanding activities whilst never allowing yourself to lose a sense of inner stillness and clarity in your thinking. If there is something you need to change, it is a lot easier if you have accurate information about what you are doing. When you can reduce the activity in your nervous system to a minimum, this becomes possible.

How to Change

How many sports psychologists does it take to change a light bulb? Just the one, but the bulb has to want to be changed! If you want to improve on what you are doing, you will have to accept that you need to change. This can be tougher than it sounds. How many New Year's resolutions have you made and broken before the week is out? You cannot change an aspect of your behaviour without changing yourself! (One of these days I will give up chocolate – honest.)

Just as importantly, you need to know what it is you are going to change; but I believe it is counterproductive to have in mind what you are going to change to! This may at first sound odd, and contradict conventional advice, but it could limit your potential if you have a set target in mind. Remember, change involves going into the unknown, moving on to somewhere you have yet to go, so how do you know where this place is? You may have ideals in mind such as, injury-free sport, a target weight, or a sub four-minute mile, but these are the destinations – not the journey that will take you there.

I believe to make successful changes that will get you moving onwards and upwards, it is vital to keep an open mind as if conducting an experiment with yourself as the subject under investigation. You must take no preconceptions into your investigations as you will limit your findings, and probably succeed only in doing more of the same thing you have always done – that is, in your comfortable habitual manner. If you can remain detached and indifferent to the process you will stand a better chance of identifying what needs to change.

> *"Keep your mind open: keep your body and movements as free as possible. An open mind is not one that is easily filled with every bit of nonsense that is current. It is one that has not fixed on concrete ideas about anything, a mind that reflects, seeks, and basically, yearns for knowledge, improvement, success, and in the case of the last lets nothing stand in the way of achievement, leaves no stone unturned, no experiment untried."*

> Percy Cerutty, pioneering running coach

Let's return to our golfer to see how he could manage this process. He knows he is pulling an unacceptable percentage of his drives but has not as yet discovered why. Thanks to his coaching sessions, he now has an idea that it is something he has started to do prior to the shot; an outside observer will always see things we cannot ourselves.

His problem is that he lacks the self-awareness and observational skills to determine what this thing is. His coach has identified that the problem is due to the tension in his shoulders, but he cannot feel this for himself and is therefore unable to stop doing it (how can you stop doing something you can't feel you are doing?) The tension in his shoulders has become part of his preparation for the swing. As soon as he thinks about playing he applies this tension and won't start the swing phase until it is present. This feeling is his template or foundation for the technique, so he won't be aware of the tension because it is there before he starts to observe his preparation. He needs to change his concept, not the end product – his technique.

So, first he has to learn to stop and rediscover his natural poise and reset his template (matrix.) He has to learn to stop and lower the level of activity in his nervous system to an appropriate minimum for each action. If he can get himself into the moment and focus on his breathing, muscle tension and position before he even picks up his club, he will be able to recognise when he starts to build up tension in his shoulders.

Now he has a chance to prevent this. By maintaining a stillness, he has learnt from 'stopping' that he can allow himself to play the shot that has been there all along. With a new understanding of his body his confidence will grow as he starts to minimize the discrepancy between his intent and his outcome – skill. Using your intellect to identify, assess and overcome a problem will give your confidence a huge boost. It is also a process to apply to any aspect of your game or even your life.

Attempts to change a technique without altering your underlying habits and concepts do not lead to real change; it's just re-arranging the furniture. It may look different on the surface but the basic building blocks will be the same; that is, your concept of effort and your movement matrix will remain the same.

A Window of Opportunity

If something has gone wrong then obviously you are going to want to make changes. However, habits that have taken a lifetime to accumulate are not going to give up without a fight. Habit is a term we use often and it has numerous connotations; but what are habits?

Habits are conditioned reflexes or learnt behaviours that practically have become automatic responses. Most people are familiar with Pavlov's experiment with dogs; in fact conditioned reflexes are often referred to as Pavlovian reflexes. Pavlov rang a bell before feeding his dogs. As dogs salivate in anticipation of eating, before long the sound of the bell became the stimulus for the dogs to start salivating because they knew the food would follow shortly. Pavlov had effectively hard-wired a response to the stimulus of the ringing bell.

From a physiological viewpoint, habits are strong neural connections within the brain. The more a neuron carries a signal the stronger the connection becomes. The Chinese have a saying that sums up the process beautifully and that is, habits are cobwebs at first, cables at last. The more you do something in response to a particular stimulus, the quicker you become at reacting, by doing the same in similar situations. This is known as the stimulus-response chain and can serve us well in many cases. However, you can become better at doing things badly! When you need to make a change and get rid of a habit, the strong cable-like connections in the brain are far more ready to react to the input generated by a stimulus than go down an as-yet untried route. Habit pathways are six-lane motorways whilst anything else is a windy, uneven footpath through a forest. Which one would you choose for a fast journey?

In the case of our golfer, just the thought of playing the shot (stimulus) would trigger the build up of tension in his neck and shoulders (habitual response.) Once the thought has entered his head that he is about to play a shot, it is too late to change anything. The response has already happened, kicking off a chain reaction running through to the completion of the stroke. He has to make the change before he thinks about playing his shot. He needs to be in the moment and fully aware of his actions to prevent unnecessary preparations. Quite simply, he needs to keep saying no to the idea that he is getting ready to play his shot.

The Split Second Workout

What is different when you are switched on, alert and in control, compared with when you are preoccupied and oblivious to what is happening around you? For example, you may have experienced walking into a room and being taken completely by surprise to see someone you hadn't expected to be there. Your first reaction is shock as your startle pattern kicks in. You will inhale involuntarily, tense your muscles and freeze momentarily. Yet on another occasion you may have reacted more to your guests' liking by greeting them in the accepted way. The difference between these two situations is, in the first instance your mind was elsewhere and you were not in the moment or focused on your present activity. The sudden unexpected appearance jolted you back into the moment. You were unable to control your reaction because it had already happened before you had the chance to choose how you would want to respond. You reacted (automatically without thought) instead of responding (considered) to the situation. When you are in the moment and focused on your present activities, you remain aware and able to control and choose how you respond.

Experiments have found that we have approximately one third of a second to control our response and if we miss this opportunity, our habitual hard-wired reaction is triggered (Libbet and Haggard). Not long, is it? These habitual reactions include those of your muscles getting ready in anticipation before you act. If you recall the experiment you tried earlier of getting out of a chair, you may have found your neck, shoulder or back muscles adopting their set pattern for the movement before you even started to move. This process is fast and very useful if your habitual reaction is suited to the situation; but what happens if it is not? You probably wouldn't know, as with the chair experiment, until your performance starts to suffer or the injuries become more frequent and serious.

This is where the ability to get into and stay in the moment really pays off. You have a sense of being in control, because there is a continuous internal dialogue with yourself as to what is happening and how you are responding. You can practically 'see the stimulus coming' and therefore cannot be caught out or be unprepared. This gives you the sense of having more time to respond, because you consciously occupy that third of a second window between the outside world and your internal response. This may sound like hard work, but remember, once you get into the moment this process takes care of itself. You don't have to do it! If you can achieve this state when playing your sport your performance will be greatly enhanced.

How will you know when you have made a successful change? In my view, when you can continuously perform an act achieving your intended outcome without your previous habitual actions surfacing, you have successfully made a change. Also when you can consciously choose how you are going to react, you have broken the knee-jerk reaction habit. A trap many people fall into is once they believe they have got something right, they have to cling to that feeling and not want to change anything. The result is no further development. If you can maintain an approach of continuous experimentation you will continue to develop and change for the better. What is right for you now will probably not be right for you next month.

Many Happy Returns

Well hopefully, this would be only once! On your return to training think as a beginner for the first few training sessions and use them to assess your technique from a detached point of view. When you were a beginner you had the building blocks – that is, how you moved your arm or leg – but not the structure of your sports techniques. It may have been that your basic building blocks were not as efficient as they could have been, as discussed in previous chapters. Putting them together to execute the techniques needed for your sport may have put stresses on your joints or muscles if they were not coordinated appropriately.

By going back to the start with your new level of self-awareness you can assess whether your basics were suitable. You will have ingrained habits associated with your techniques that will feel right, but if these were habits that caused your injury or loss of form it really won't help to repeat them – especially with more effort – in the belief that you are not trying hard enough.

One advantage of recovering from an injury is that it can provide you with instant feedback concerning your performance. It is like an alarm bell that rings if you are doing it in your habitual manner, i.e., wrong again. If the bell rings, STOP! Stop immediately what you are doing and give yourself a few moments to get back into the moment by focusing on the action of your breathing (remember not to do this – just observe,) your balance and the ground underneath your feet. Run some checks to see if you are holding any tension, starting from the jaw and neck and working your way down. These thoughts will lower the level of activity and bring you back to a state of inner stillness.

When you have achieved this, maintain your awareness in the moment for a while longer before starting your activity again. Immediately you recognise something that tightens your body and prevents a feeling of lightness in your movement, stop and go back to the beginning. It is tempting to carry on with the niggles or aches and pains – I know I've done this enough in the past, but as mentioned earlier, all you will achieve by doing more of the same thing is the same end result – the injury.

Remember that the urge to do things in your old familiar way will be strong because the pathways in your brain are strong. Get used to things feeling wrong – just like when you folded your arms in the opposite way. If it feels wrong or different it definitely is not your old habitual way of doing it. This doesn't mean you instantly will be right, but if you can rid yourself of the urge to do it right you will at least allow for a new way to come about – that is, a change. By taking the habitual brake off you can let your body, with its inbuilt mechanisms for movement and coordination, work things out. Detach yourself from the 'doing bit' and allow yourself to focus on the decision-making. You are the captain of the ship – not the guy who turns the wheel or shovels the coal.

Conclusion

If something has gone wrong is it likely due to something you are already doing wrong. This sounds obvious but remember it probably won't feel wrong because you will have been doing it for some time as you operate within your self-styled matrix. These habits are very familiar to you and will feel comfortable, making you believe there is no other way to move. Yet until you can perform without them you won't recognise the poor influence of these habits. Making changes to your technique or approach without first stopping and addressing your habitual patterns will have a limited outcome. Lower the level of 'noise' in your system, and your sensitivity to what is actually happening in your body will improve. Learning how to stop will reset your awareness threshold to a lower level, allowing you to pick up more that previously would have gone unnoticed. Now you will have more accurate information about what you are doing, giving you a better chance to observe and act accordingly to make the necessary changes.

The challenge now becomes one of increasing your awareness and skills to get you into the moment, to train smarter and not to keep pushing yourself harder doing the same things. Continuous improvement and development come from self-observation, mindful training and a desire to learn from your endeavours. Don't just be satisfied with improvements to the tangible performance measures; always look to develop your understanding of yourself and it will become a life-long study.

9 Living In The Zone

When you change into your kit you do not suddenly acquire a new body ready to face the demands of your sport. What you do with your body outside of your sport will have an impact on how you perform. Aside from the obvious things such as your diet and other lifestyle choices, how you move and carry yourself in your car, at your desk or during other leisure pursuits will condition your body. It is unreasonable to believe otherwise, because you will always spend more time away from your training than actually doing it.

If you can accept that two hours training will condition your body in a specific way, what about the other sixteen waking hours? How do your daily activities influence your body and more importantly, your body concept? Do you collapse into your armchair when you get home? Are you standing up straight by tightening your back or holding your stomach in? These actions will influence how you move when running for the finish line, teeing off or trying to defend a breakpoint with your second serve, just as much as your specific training. Yet how much attention do you pay to these everyday activities?

You can practise being in the moment and focusing on the present in any situation. The next time you have one of those necessary mundane routine tasks to perform such as emptying the dishwasher, see if you can focus and be in the moment. Where are you bending from to reach down to retrieve the plates? Are you aware of the movement when squatting or is your mind elsewhere? Sense the contact you have with the floor, the plates and kitchen units. Be conscious of your decision-making process of what to get out next, the order and where you are putting things. This may sound trivial and even dull; but what are you usually thinking about when doing this? When your mind is elsewhere during the necessary daily tasks you will rush them and get nothing from the activity. Make an effort to be in the moment and you will get a totally different experience of reality. If you can do it here, it will help when you are on the home straight. It's the same process.

Often the first response of people coming to one of my sessions is, "do I have to be focused like this all the time? I don't know whether I could think like this all day." Good observation, I don't think I could either. However the important point is that with practice you will start to develop the skill to choose whether to be in the moment of not. You are thinking all the time now, so it requires no extra effort. You will be thinking about many things and probably half the time, about nothing related to your current situation. You wouldn't dream of playing tennis without working on your backhand so why not work on your ability to focus and on self-awareness skills away from your game? A small shift in your focus, requiring no extra effort, can bring a significant improvement to your performance.

- To get into The Zone you need to be focused fully on the activity

- To focus you will have to be in the moment

- To get into the moment you need to be fully conscious of your surroundings, what you sense, and your reactions

- To achieve all this you have to practise!

So whether you are about to take a penalty or open your front door, practise being conscious of what you are doing and it will become easier to get into the moment.

The Discovery Zone

I often have difficulty convincing people that by developing their ability to be fully present in the moment, they will improve their fitness. How is this? Well, first let's look at what fitness means. It's not all about stamina, suppleness and strength because you could have all of these qualities and still be hopeless at sport. Fitness means being able to do what you want to do, when you want to do it, and to do it well. Your level of fitness is therefore judged by how well you perform at your chosen activity. A tri-athlete makes very different demands on her body compared with those of a weightlifter or sprinter; but one common skill they all require is the ability to make appropriate decisions - and not just during competition. When do I train? What do I do for that training session? What do I focus on? And just as important, when do I rest? How many athletes sustain injuries by over-training or doing the wrong sort of training?

Just being the fittest player on the pitch won't make you the best. You have to work on when and how to make your move, read the game and second-guess your opponent - and you must know what techniques to use and when. So how do you train in this skill? There is no substitute for experience. You just can't teach that because you must be able to observe what actions deliver the best outcomes, and this can only be done by trial and error. However, you can optimise your learning opportunities by being in the right state of mind.

You have probably experienced days when you can pick up a new concept right away whereas on others, you may struggle to make sense of what should be easy. One moment you are coming to terms with Einstein's theory of relativity, the next you are struggling to operate the toaster! It has happened to me. Does this discrepancy sound familiar? Of course it does. You were either in the moment or on another planet. Learning is so much easier when you are in the moment because your brain is synchronised; you are hyper alert and as an added bonus, you have time to analyse what you see and appear to have longer to decide what to do. Also, you will not be as susceptible to your automatic habitual reactions taking over and robbing you of the chance to try something different and assess its effectiveness.

It is always worthwhile asking, "how do I benefit from my training?" Of course you will be keeping fit, in shape and hopefully enjoying the time you train as long as you are applying some intelligence to the process. But what are you actually learning from training that will help to make you a better person?

I am sure you have all met those self-obsessed gym junkies – in fact I was one of them for many years! When I look back I find it difficult to determine what I gained from all my 'no pain, no gain' training that benefits me now. Yes, I could say I learnt from my mistakes – eventually, but it took a long time to eradicate the poor habits I had developed during those years. Of course, I could still be paying for it with undetected habits lurking beneath the surface. And there were definitely few true Zone moments. What I did achieve was a certain skill for injuring myself. I wasted all that effort because I did not apply my analytical skills as a computer programmer to my training. I cut myself in two. I switched off the thinking part when I changed into my sports kit and blindly followed the fitness fad of the day.

When you are in The Zone you are better placed to learn and remember. This explains why most can recall with clarity their Zone moments many years later. If The Zone experience is related to being in alpha state as discussed in Chapter 2, this is known to improve synchronicity between the various brain centres and therefore increase learning function. Increasing our time in The Zone therefore enhances our ability, as we learn more quickly; but more importantly, it lays down reliable, efficient skill patterns without the inappropriate muscular activities we associate with poor performances. If it feels effortless, it's a good one!

East verses West

You may already use structured ways to get into The Zone such as yoga, tai chi, martial arts, Zen or meditation. In the East they recognised the importance of being focused on the present centuries ago. The Japanese tea ceremony is not about drinking tea; it's an activity to become absorbed in the present. Yoga and the martial arts have been practiced in the west for years now but in many cases I believe the original philosophy has been forgotten. 'Westernised' versions of these disciplines fail to appreciate that the benefits are in the mindful practice and attention to detail, and in the 'physical' techniques themselves.

A good example of this is yoga breathing 'exercises'. These procedures are not directly meant to improve your breathing but to provide a technique to focus on the present. Originally they were not taught to beginners until they had reached a high level of understanding and competence. The means is often seen as the end - that is, the breathing movements are treated as an exercise rather than as a process to get into the moment. Yoga is then reduced to an exercise or relaxation system rather than a philosophy for lifelong study. This is evident in the increase of 'yoga injuries' as people compete with others in the class to get the best position. Obviously in these cases little attention is given to the process and the moment, as the end position becomes the target. If we take the philosophy out of the practice it becomes just a series of movements without substance.

You are what you eat

You are also only as good as your last meal! Sports nutrition has rightly attained a high priority in any serious athlete's training program. But aside from the obvious consideration of energy input and release, it is also known that certain substances found in foods help to release neurotransmitters within the brain. For instance, phenylalanine found in meat, eggs, grains and soybeans is used to make dopamine, a neurotransmitter that affects brain processes controlling movement, emotion and ability to experience pain and pleasure. Tryptophan found in meat, diary, bananas and eggs is involved in the manufacture of serotonin, the feel good neurotransmitter.

There are over one hundred thousand chemical reactions occurring in the brain every second, so balance is vital. Perhaps you have experienced a time when you got this wrong when training after a heavy meal or eating junk food. You may have a sense of feeling lethargic, having little energy and no ability to focus. Your chances to get into The Zone can be greatly enhanced by eating the right foods. However, every individual can respond differently to the same food, so it is worth getting professional advice or experimenting to find what works for you.

Staying With The Program

Your training and sport should be viewed as part of your personal development and not as a separate physical activity. Many individuals regard their sport and exercise as a way of taking a break from their intellectual pursuits and train their 'mental' and 'physical' self separately. However, do you really perform at best by splitting yourself in two? Does taking the 'mind' out of physical activity result in mindless action? Skills and abilities learnt from participating in your sport can translate back to your personal and professional life; it also works the other way around.

If you are going to get the full benefit from all of the hours you devote to training, it has to be a challenge otherwise it becomes just another everyday routine. The reason many people fail to achieve their ambitions is because their training has become monotonous. Once the initial enthusiasm has gone, what have you got left? If your training program consists of repetitions of conventional exercises, how do you motivate yourself to keep going back?

Yes, there are those who can stick with a strict routine if they keep a clear goal in mind to give them the reason to train. However, I would argue that a conventional exercise routine does not necessarily provide you with the sort of challenge that would unite your whole self into learning a skill really worth doing. Exercise routines do have the elements necessary for a Zone experience, but is being able to do five hundred sit-ups as rewarding as hitting your first hole-in-one? Both require effort and commitment but I would argue that five hundred sit-ups a day will not prove any real worth – I know because I used to do that many! So whilst you may take satisfaction from the process of achieving an ambition, how will the actual activity benefit you and your sport? When I stopped doing all those sit-ups my flexibility and stamina improved as it became easier to move and breathe without all that tension in the abdominal muscles.

I would say the main difference between an exercise routine and a sport is the element of learning a skill. Back in Chapter 2 we looked at why being able to do something well is rewarding because it gives us status within a group. Of course being able to hit a hole-in-one may not reward humanity in such a tangible way as discovering a cure for cancer. However, it does demonstrate our potential for progression and self-mastery that will earn the respect of your peers and motivate others to higher achievements.

You may argue that you still need exercises to condition your body for your sport. That's fine, but do approach your exercises with the same mindful attitude that you would apply to your sport. If you use exercise routines, check that you are not learning poor movement habits from doing exercises that have nothing in common with 'natural' activity. A sit-up is a good example of this. How does the sit-up help your body for your sport? You will develop strong abdominal muscles but only for doing sit-ups. When do you need to use them like that in your sport? Exercise programs can be an important part of your training but only if they encourage good movement and can be used for developing your ability to focus and improve your body knowledge.

Your training program will never become a chore if you approach it as a total activity for personal development; train consciously; and set the right goals.

Avoiding The Training Trap

I see too many people who are either getting injured or frustrated by their results, due to a misapplication of effort or misdirected focus. They don't lack ambition or the determination to succeed, because they know what they want and are prepared to devote substantial time to get it. What they do lack is the ability to be flexible in their approach, and that's because of the guiding influence of strong habits developed by long hours of repetitive training. Remember, practice makes permanent, not perfect!

I have met athletes, whose hopes have been dashed in one sport due to injury, move onto another only to sustain a new injury. Each time they change sport they will throw themselves into the training in exactly the same way that got them injured previously. It's not the sport at fault; it's their approach. However until they can overcome the habits that got them into this state nothing will change.

One such highly motivated athlete I taught had competed at international and national level in four separate sports as one injury after another forced a change. No one could question her commitment or ability to learn new skills, but she had failed to notice why she kept getting seriously injured. If you crashed your car three times it would not make sense to go and buy a new one and expect the problem to go away. The appropriate action would be to sign up for a course of lessons and brush up on your driving skills.

It is easy to develop tunnel vision and only see where you want to be. Remember the young Japanese boy who wanted to become a martial arts master, who failed to appreciate the importance of the journey? See your sport as a means of achieving life-long self-improvement and look to learn from your training regardless of the outcome. Failures and setbacks may be temporarily disheartening, but they really do provide you with a learning opportunity. Dealing with these situations will strengthen your resolve and develop your ability to adapt and move on.

If you are a competitive athlete your career should not become a source for frustration with thoughts for what could have been, or worse still, the origin of a serious injury that will prevent you enjoying physical activity after retirement.

Play your sport well and you will get fit! It doesn't have to be repetitive and dull. If you are enjoying what you are doing you double the benefit as the connections from your brain to your muscles are strengthened by your primitive survival mechanisms. After all, fitness is an ability that used to keep us alive long before the gym was invented!

A Way Forward

Getting better at what you do is a great motivator and can keep you training and active throughout your life. How you judge your performance will change along with your priorities. Treat your training as an important part of your life and your will get more in return. I would advise the following actions:

1   Write down your goals and how you are going to get there.

2   Keep a training diary.

3   Take up a new sport or activity to complement your chosen sport. Use your new challenge to apply these techniques; this will be easier because you will have fewer habits associated with it.

4   Assess and experiment with your diet.

5   Never be afraid to challenge conventional thinking. How do the experts know they are right? Hopefully, most of the time they will be, but you may be basing your training philosophy on the 'facts' they have got wrong. It doesn't matter if you turn out to be wrong, because you will have come to the right way by your own experimentation and investigations.

6   Find an Alexander Technique teacher and try a few lessons. They will be able to show you things that no other coach or therapist has shown you before. You might just find a whole new perspective opening up before you.

7   Keep an open mind.

8   Train without judging your performance – if it's bad ask why, but don't beat yourself up about it.

9   Make your objective for each training session to be in the moment and from there allow yourself to slip into The Zone.

10 And lastly, remember you can practise being in the moment at any time of day, even away from your sport.

No longer will your training be just about winning or achieving personal bests, although these are not to be dismissed as meaningless. It will become a life-long pursuit of applying your skills and wits against the challenges that sport can throw at you. Maintain a child-like curiosity about your body and how it works, and adopt an attitude that your training is about self-improvement on all levels. That will bring rewards far exceeding the more obvious physical benefits.

THE END

Index

Printed in the United Kingdom
by Lightning Source UK Ltd.
127451UK00002B/201/A

9 781905 823062